HIGH ROLLERS

Fly Fishing
for Giant Tarpon

T0243703

BILL BISHOP

STACKPOLE
BOOKS

Essex, Connecticut
Blue Ridge Summit, Pennsylvania

STACKPOLE BOOKS

An imprint of Globe Pequot, the trade division of
The Rowman & Littlefield Publishing Group, Inc.
4501 Forbes Blvd., Ste. 200
Lanham, MD 20706
www.rowman.com

Distributed by NATIONAL BOOK NETWORK

Copyright © 2009 by Headwater Books
Stackpole Books paperback edition published in 2024

Art by Bill Bishop
Photography by Mark Hatter

British Library Cataloguing in Publication Information available

Library of Congress Cataloging-in-Publication Data available

LCCN: 2008938343

ISBN 9780811775403 (paperback)
ISBN 9781461751120 (epub)

♾™ The paper used in this publication meets the minimum requirements of
American National Standard for Information Sciences—Permanence of Paper
for Printed Library Materials, ANSI/NISO Z39.48-1992.

Contents

Acknowledgments   v

Foreword   vi

Introduction   vii

CHAPTER 1   Battle!   1

CHAPTER 2   Biology and Behavior   7

CHAPTER 3   Leaders and Connections   19

CHAPTER 4   Flies   33

CHAPTER 5   Skiffs   45

CHAPTER 6   Running the Boat   57

CHAPTER 7   The Hunt   67

CHAPTER 8   Body Language   79

CHAPTER 9   Staying in the Game   87

CHAPTER 10 Casting   93

CHAPTER 11 Feeding Fish   99

CHAPTER 12 Hook-Sets   113

CHAPTER 13 Fighting Fish   117

CHAPTER 14 Safe Landings   135

CHAPTER 15 Reflections   143

Index   149

This book is dedicated to Janie. I got hooked on her in 1965. We tied the knot in '68. It must have been a good one. Forty years is a good run in anybody's book, but we're just getting underway.

Acknowledgments

Some of those who have played a critical role in the writing of this book will be revealed throughout its pages. I am grateful to all of them, whether I mention them or not. Lefty Kreh heads the list. From day one, he has provided me with wise counsel and constant encouragement. The beginnings of this treasured friendship can be traced directly to Flip Pallot. I never would have met Lefty without him. Sharing the deck of a skiff with these two icons is indescribable.

Much of what I know about tarpon fishing is a result of Tommy Locke's countless observant hours logged atop the poling platform. I deeply appreciate his willingness and ability to pass it on. Pat Fulford and Charlie Madden have played a large role in my tarpon-fishing life and our countless exchanges of concepts and ideas have proven invaluable. Their knack for humor has made the learning process thus far that much more enjoyable. Another person who has been critical to the final outcome of this effort is my editor and friend, Jay Nichols. Just as teamwork is

the key to catching tarpon, it's critical in a project such as this. We managed to squeeze a bit of fishing in with the work. The photography of Mark Hatter is nothing short of spectacular. It takes a consummate angler peering through the view finder to capture what he has.

My family has been beyond supportive. My children have been a constant source of inspiration, and it's perfectly fitting that this book is dedicated to my wife, Janie. Lastly, my father has provided unfailing support and keen insight, but that pales in the face of his greatest impact on this book and my life. He always made time to take me fishing and hunting. My passion for the outdoors is a gift from him.

Foreword

Flip Pallot introduced me to Bill Bishop. During my long life I have been one of the luckiest of fly fishermen because I have spent so much time with so many wonderful people. Driving back to the airport with Flip after spending time with Bill Bishop, I said to him, "Flip, you have introduced me to many amazing people. Of all of them I've met in the past few years, Bill Bishop is my favorite."

There are many reasons for this. Bill is a family man who loves his wife, children, and grandkids (for God's sake don't ask him about his grandkids). He loves to laugh and he is the kind of friend everyone wants to have.

Like so many of my friends he is obsessed with fly rodding for tarpon—and he is among the half dozen best I know. One of the reasons for his ability to find and catch so many fish is that he constantly wants to improve. He reminds me of vacuum cleaner, sucking up as much information as he can. He is always looking for a better way.

This is a different book. Most fly-fishing books fall either into the category of how-to or what I call "pretty writing." This book has great writing—even some one-liners I never heard and will steal. The text is filled with emotion that any serious tarpon fishermen will feel. The photos really explain how exciting fishing for these silver giants can be.

I knew Bill could draw but the many illustrations in the book not only dress it up and explain things better, but they help the reader understand why people get so hooked on tarpon.

The section on tackle is the result of too many trips to count for these silver giants and is as good as it gets. Bill's knot drawings are superb. Bill is an innovator—one look at his tarpon skiff will show you that—and readers will learn many things from his time on the water and his ingenuity.

I consider this beautifully written and illustrated how-to book essential reading for anyone interested in chasing these wonderful fish—the high rollers.

—Lefty Kreh

Introduction

In 1999, when I was forty-nine, a heart attack stopped me in my tracks. After many years of working hard as a salesman and raising a family who were now out of the house and raising families of their own, I was just at a point where I had freedom to fish more. The first night I spent in the hospital, I couldn't muster the strength to crawl to the toilet, and the idea of standing on the deck of my skiff fighting a tarpon seemed like a pipe dream. The windows of opportunity that had recently opened had slammed shut in the blink of an eye.

A few months before, my good friend Keith Holcomb told me: "There's something definite and final about writing down your goals and dreams." Though that seemed like a good idea, I didn't do it. Now, it seemed necessary. I asked the nurse to bring me a pad and pen, and I started writing. When I finished, I had scrawled twenty-five goals down on the page, and I was bound and determined to accomplish every one of them.

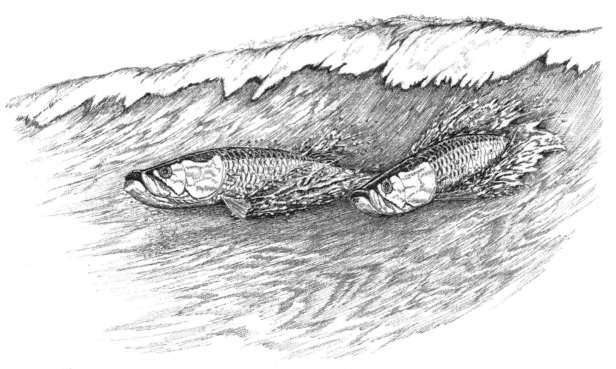

Laughing with friends is a huge part of what makes tarpon fishing so enjoyable. Above, good friend David Olson jumps a nice tarpon. MARK HATTER PHOTO

Here are the things on the list that involved fishing.

1. Get in good physical condition.
2. Catch a 200-pound tarpon on 16-pound-test.
3. Catch a 100-pound tarpon on 6-pound-test.
4. Catch a 150-pound tarpon on 8-pound-test.
5. Catch a blue marlin on fly.
6. Build a wood skiff.
7. Write and illustrate a book on tarpon fishing.
8. Catch a 20-pound snook on fly.

Here's number seven.

Only a few books devoted entirely to tarpon have been written. All of the ones that I am aware of are written by people who have spent their fair share of time on the flats, and they all offer valuable information to readers. Mine is not meant to replace any of them. It may be presumptuous of me to think that I know enough about tarpon to help people catch them more effectively, but I fish for tarpon a lot and believe I have a different approach and perspective that might help you catch more fish.

This book is most of what I know about tarpon, but it's not the complete story or even everything I'll know when I'm done fishing. The learning curve never flattens out and questions and answers are buried in each outing. At the end of the day, small lessons learned on the water are like loose change tossed in a jar on the dresser. Individually, they might not amount to much, but together they add up to something worthwhile.

When I first started to learn how to fish for tarpon, friends shared what they knew with me, which helped me learn a lot faster. One of my goals in this book is to help others learn about this sport a little quicker and to cut some time off the learning process. Although I believe that getting out on the water and figuring things out for yourself is the best way to learn, the friendships you make along the way by helping others is one of the greatest things our sport has to offer.

In fact, at least for me, laughing with friends is a huge part of what makes this sport enjoyable. So this book is both my best effort to share with you what I have learned about how to catch these magnificent fish and also a celebration of my partners—some who I fish with and some, such as my wife, who I don't. But all of them make every day, on the water and off, better.

CHAPTER ONE

Battle!

An hour into the fight, I needed help. Flip Pallot listened intently to my Mayday as he drove to the post office from his home in Mims: "I'm in the lagoon hooked to a huge 'poon on 6-pound . . . need help!" Flip made a U-turn in his truck and drove to LeFiles fish camp in Oak Hill.

I hooked up at 9:00 AM, and the fight up until that point amounted to nothing more than trying to keep fly line on the reel while simultaneously managing the skiff. At that point I was nothing more to the tarpon than a nuisance, and I imagined that I must have felt to her like it feels when I have something caught in my teeth. Annoying, persistent, and present—but nothing to get worked up about. She was a surefire world record for the 6-pound class. I guessed her weight to be 120 pounds, so I figured there was more than ample wiggle room. Stu Apte held the record on 6-pound-test with an 82-pound, 8-ounce fish.

That morning, the water was slick calm when I made the 5-mile run from my dock to Mosquito Lagoon well before first light. As I motored slowly around the flat searching for rolling fish, I noticed the tip of her tail protruding above the surface of

the flat water just ahead and to my starboard. She was facing away. I cut the power to the bow-mounted trolling motor and drifted the skiff slightly past her and 20 feet out. I could make out the outline of her frame resting motionless in the dark, stained water.

I made the short cast, keeping the rod as low to the water as possible. The fly landed 2 feet off her nose, and one pump of her tail telegraphed her intent to eat. To prepare for the gentle set, I reminded myself out loud, like I always do, "You are fishing 6-pound." Normal hook-setting methods will break the thin line instantly, and without the reminder it's easy to attempt to drive the point in using the backbone of the rod. Using 6- and 8-pound requires feeling the fish through your hands and setting with the rod tip. As I fed the fish, I held my rod tip at a 45-degree angle to the water to help protect the leader, much like you would for freshwater trout.

Because manufacturers did not produce hooks specifically for hooking tarpon on light tippet, I had improvised by clipping the bent portion of the end of a #1 thin-wire circle hook with wire

1

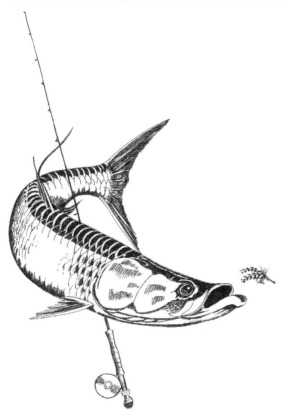

cutters and filing a new point to the blunt end. This gave me the wider gap needed for large fish and a thin wire that could penetrate the tarpon's bony jaw.

The fly stayed high in the water column just ahead of the tarpon. When she ate and turned, I simply left the rod at that position and pulled down with my line hand with several short, quick jerks. As she spun to the right, away from the skiff, the hook found a home.

The first jumps were heart-stopping, and after each one I was relieved to still feel pressure on the line. Managing to keep a tarpon stuck beyond the first miracle minute is just as difficult as driving the hook home. Though I had built elasticity into the rig by using a one-hundred-turn Bimini twist on the upper portion of the knot (a trick Lefty had taught me), fighting a large tarpon on nothing

more than a wisp of a tippet is a delicate, perhaps even foolhardy, proposition.

Jay Dixon and a companion were fishing in the area and were kind enough to deliver Flip to the deck of my skiff. The boys were thrilled to meet a fishing hero. My confidence of landing the tarpon soared as Flip stepped aboard, a rescue paramount to Muhammad Ali joining me in a bar fight. "She doesn't stand a chance," we celebrated.

The endurance test ("fight" is not really accurate) went all day and into the night. I tried my best to not do more than the leader could withstand but at the same time do enough to eventually take a toll on the tarpon. This game went on without intermission and began to take its toll on everyone.

I was using the lightest drag setting possible. As the fish ate up more line and backing, I backed off even more on the drag, because the drag actually increases as the spool diameter becomes smaller. I had cut away some of the running line before rigging. Six- or eight-pound-test tippet can break easily under the pressure of fish dragging yards of fly line and backing through the water, especially when there is a bow in the line. On long runs, I elevated the rod as much as possible to lift as much line out of the water as I could.

Our celebration idled down. I had assured Janie before leaving the house that I'd be home in time to drive her and our daughter, Shannon, to the airport (they were due to catch an early flight to Bermuda that day), but it didn't look like I was going to make it. We could have taken the fish several times with a kill gaff if we'd had one. She managed to stay just out of reach. With each passing lightning storm, I wanted Janie to know we made

The first jumps were heart-stopping, and after each one I was relieved to still feel pressure on the line. MARK HATTER PHOTO

it, and Flip's wife had to be wondering how long those lines were at the post office. We called everyone in the state trying desperately to locate a kill gaff. The batteries in our phones ran out. Where's more drinking water and food when you need it?

Word of our encounter got out, and strangers showed up in the black of night with food and much-needed water, but no kill gaff. My son, Billy, drove from Orlando, launched his skiff, and signed on as bartender and captain of the cheerleading squad. I was sworn to sobriety for the duration of the fight. Friend and local guide Scott Tripp raced to the lagoon the instant he heard. The fact he was grilling dinner for a dozen guests didn't slow him down in the least. He didn't have a kill gaff on board either. At some point I recall Billy anchoring his skiff and boarding Scott's. It sounded like a great party as they followed behind us. Midnight came and went.

I had never seen as much fire in the water as that night. Every movement encased the tarpon in a dome of iridescent light. The sight of it took me back to my childhood when my Dad and I would make predawn runs to Stump Pass. I would perch in the stern of the wood skiff, staring with great wonder and delight at the brightly lit pair of cresting waves fading far back in the wake.

We were all tired. The tarpon, Flip, and I had crossed the fifteen-hour mark. The feeling in my hands came and went. At times, I would gaze at the fly rod in my grasp, but it seemed like someone else was holding it. Flip steered the tiller of the outboard. It was the same for him. The tarpon had waxed and waned, but her heading never changed—due north, straight up the intra-coastal waterway.

Strenuous battles with tarpon were not new to me, but this one was pushing the envelope. Aside from the fight with the fish, I was waging an inner battle. I was hesitant to do too much with too little. Six-pound is but a thread with such a fish. Just as consuming, I feared not doing enough to close the deal. It's easy to fall on either side of the ledger when so many people are going to such great lengths to make a personal dream possible. I had my friends in my corner. The tarpon was on her own.

Some anglers frown on fighting tarpon on 6- and 8-pound-test because of the added stress on the fish due to the longer and more strenuous battles, which can also make the fish more susceptible to shark attacks. So how worried was I that tarpon would keel over and die? Frankly, after the first ten hours or so, I think it would have been the sporting thing for her to do.

There was no horizon separating the water from the night sky. We were idling north because she did. Channel markers came and faded away in the darkness. There were few lights burning in the windows of the houses sprinkled along the river. It was late. Distance and length were unfathomable, but somewhere ahead appeared unfamiliar puffs of misty light that showed bright and then quickly faded away like miniature fireworks. I was relieved to hear Flip ask, "What the hell is that?" I had never seen anything like it before.

I didn't dare turn around to look, but I am positive Flip was scratching his beard. He always does this when he ponders. With a tone of discovery, he finally announced, "Porpoise!" There were three together, each coming south. With every exhale, misty geysers of phosphorescent light fired aloft and rapidly dissipated. I can still see it when I close my eyes. In the narrow channel they were sure to pass by the tarpon—and then the skiff—but they didn't do both. The trio turned in formation on a tight axis just off the bow and adjacent to the tarpon. They steered immediately alongside her starboard and port. "They're going to run into the leader," I said.

"Porpoise don't accidentally run into much of anything," Flip assured me. I put my trust in the countless days and nights Flip has logged on the water in every corner of the world. He was right. Porpoise don't hit things accidentally!

Now the light around them was intense due to the added activity in the water. They darted over

They darted over her back and under her belly like aviators inspecting the damage of a wounded bomber desperately trying to make it home.

her back and under her belly like aviators inspecting the damage of a wounded bomber desperately trying to make it home. This continued for a quarter of an hour.

I don't know what occurred during those fifteen minutes. None of us do and perhaps we're not granted that privilege. I had gathered my support team, and she had finally assembled hers. She had new friends in her corner, and it was a new ball game. Now after sixteen hours of meticulously disassembling her spirit, she reassembled her strength. We were outgunned.

Without notice, the porpoise peeled from her side, turned back to the south, and raced past the gunnels. They each rolled over as they glided by as if to get a better look at who was behind all of this. The tarpon spun, chasing in the wake of her companions, and passed down the side of the skiff. Her tail kicks were strong; and I was dead tired, and line was peeling hard off the spool. As she disappeared in the night, Flip whipped the nose of the skiff south and sped up. To no avail. I don't know if she jumped or not. Something did. We heard it where we couldn't see. The spool stopped, and the backing sagged limp on the deck. She was free to go, and so were we.

I recall with perfect clarity what happened next. Flip and I stared eye to eye, and I said, "Have you ever had a more exciting day? Thanks for all your help." I poured a Scotch. It was 1:00 AM.

Billy dropped Flip back at the fish camp. Once Flip arrived home, he fought the need for sleep and wrote down the night's events, which was later published under the title "The Longest Day and Night" in *Fly Fishing in Salt Waters.* Scott followed me home. We stopped our skiffs on the way and watched mullet splash in the phosphorescent pools of a mudflat. It was spellbinding.

Even though I was exhausted, I couldn't muster sleep after I put the skiff away. I drove to Orlando, showered, and crawled into bed at 4:00 AM. Janie asked sleepily, "Did you get her?"

"No," I answered, fading off to sleep.

I woke up with daylight pouring through the windows. There was a note on the bedside table. Without my drugstore glasses, I strained to make out the words: "Drove to the airport . . . looked like you needed sleep more than I needed a ride. I am very proud. You gave it your best. Love, Janie."

The phone rang. Thinking it was Janie still on the ground, I answered: "Hey honey."

"Honey?" Pat Fulford laughed, "You're not running around naked again are you?" Fulford's quick. He continued, "Where are you? There's lots of 'poons out here." He was in the lagoon.

"I'll see you in an hour," I replied. I drove back to the river house and dumped the skiff in the water. It wouldn't start. I checked the fuel tank. It was bone-dry, and so was I. I limped inside, stretched out, and slept until dark.

CHAPTER TWO

Biology and Behavior

The 186-pound tarpon I released last week in Homosassa was alive when I was in kindergarten, and she weighed only a few pounds then. In 1955, when I was eight, she spent her summer days surviving in the estuaries of Boca Grande while I was surviving in Englewood, only a few miles away. We learned how to swim at the same time, in the same water. In 1965, she waited out the winter in Cuba for warmer water, and I met my wife in high school. The tarpon tipped the scales at 90 pounds when our daughter, Shannon, was born, and she broke a 100 when Billy came along. And, when I had a heart attack in 1999, she dodged a hammerhead in Captiva Pass. We both got through it.

Part of the magic of tarpon fishing lies in the magic and mystery of the fish themselves. However, what you and I might call "magic," a fishery biologist would call "lack of data." One of the reasons for this lack of information about things such as migration patterns and spawning is because there is an overall lack of funds available for research. Tarpon, while part of a million-dollar sport-fishing industry, are not food fish, so beyond

anglers and a handful of biologists there is limited interest. Let's face it. It's not bothering Oprah that we do not have all the answers about tarpon migration and behavior. And, in truth, it doesn't bother me that much either, because I like the magic. But, for those interested in reading about the latest science regarding tarpon (and bonefish), consult *Biology and Management of the World's Tarpon Fisheries,* edited by Gerald Ault (CRC Press, 2007). Much of the information here was gathered from that source.

The tarpon's scientific name is *Megalops atlanticus,* which is derived from the Greek word "megalops" meaning "large-eyed," one of the tarpon's prominent features. While "large-eyed fish of the Atlantic" is a fair description, the tarpon's common names are more descriptive and befit this fish's awesome power. In Florida, it is also known as the silver king, and anyone who has tangled with one of these magnificent creatures would agree its power and strength is unmatched. Less formally, like a nickname among regulars, it goes by 'poon. In Spanish speaking countries, such as Brazil and Costa Rica, it goes by *sabalo.*

Part of the magic of tarpon fishing lies in the magic and mystery of the fish themselves. They are both beautiful and formidable opponents. MARK HATTER PHOTO

Tarpon, as their common name suggests, have large silvery scales on their sides and green or dark backs, depending on where they are caught. For instance, in Homosassa, the tarpon are often referred to as "black backs" because of the distinct differences between these fish and the typical greenish-tinged fish of the Keys and Boca Grande. Aside from the color variance, Homosassa black backs are much stockier than their cousins in the Keys and Boca Grande. Fish that live inland can have brownish coloration to their backs. They have a forked tail, common among all fish with speed and power. Their large prominent eyes (befitting a nocturnal feeder) are propped up on top of their heads like an afterthought, much like the taillights on an Edsel.

Their upturned mouth makes them look like they have an underbite. Because of this upturned mouth and the position of their eyes, tarpon typically attack their prey from under it, opening their large mouths and creating a powerful suction as the water rushes out their gills, sucking in their prey. When you hold onto a tarpon's jaw and look into its mouth, you begin to understand why it is more difficult to get a solid hookup on fly. Fine densely packed teeth line their mouth. Because of these small teeth, tarpon swallow most of their prey whole, though they will crush some prey—crabs, for instance—with their long bony plate along the lower, upturned jaw. The hard interior mouth makes it extremely difficult to penetrate with a hook, which, combined with the fish's propensity to leap, means that even when you get a tarpon to eat your fly, you have to have a lot of things going in your favor to land them. The sandpaperlike mouth is extremely abrasive, making heavier shock tippets necessary additions to your leaders.

When a tarpon rolls in the warm morning light, its scales and silver sheen are a magnificent sight. The main reason that we see them roll so frequently is because tarpon have the unique feature, at least among the world's gamefish, of being able to breathe air. Tarpon can absorb oxygen both through their gills and by breathing air when they roll, often making an audible gulping sound that can often be heard when the water is still. They store this air in a swim bladder connected to their esophagus. In areas where oxygen levels are low, tarpon roll and take air more frequently. This ability to breathe air allows them to live in oxygen poor waters such as backcountry sloughs and golf course ponds when they are juveniles. This is also the case when tarpon are traveling fast and exerting themselves. During the waning periods of an extended fight with an angler, it's typical for tarpon to take on additional air, much like we do under stress. I think tarpon also roll in response to other rolling tarpon, much the same way we yawn when watching someone else do so. Often a pair of tarpon will roll almost in tandem. The frequency of this coupled with the odds of both fish requiring additional air at the same time indicate that this might be a response to another fish rolling.

Tarpon, in addition to their keen eyesight, also have good "hearing," aided both by their lateral line and their internal swim bladder, which amplifies vibrations. It pays to keep the noise and move-

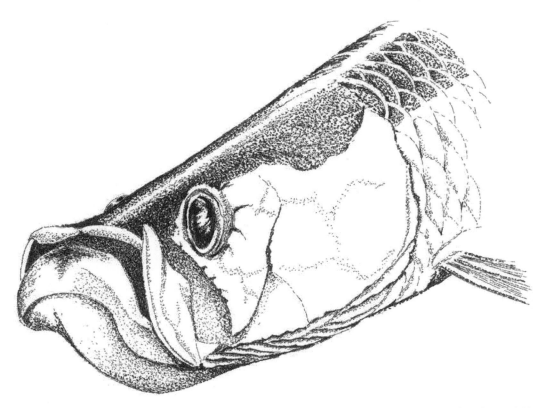

Their large prominent eyes (befitting a nocturnal feeder) are propped up on top of their heads like an afterthought, much like the taillights on an Edsel. They also have prominent upturned mouths.

Tarpon are strong fighters with plenty of endurance. You need to be physically fit to tame one quickly. MARK HATTER PHOTO

ment to a minimum when fly fishing for tarpon. An outboard (or even a trolling motor run at high speed), excessive body motion while fly casting, or waves bouncing backward off the hull from an anchored or posted skiff can all spook fish.

Tarpon are magnificent fighters. Their size, power, strength, and endurance far surpass that of most fish. As a result, don't make the mistake of thinking you can tangle with giant tarpon on a consistent basis without being physically fit. Your strength and endurance must mimic that of a 150-pound tarpon to bring her to the boat.

Despite their enormous size as adults, a tarpon's beginnings are humble. Tarpon spend the first few months of their lives as small eel-like larvae that grow to a little under 3 centimeters (going through a short phase where they actually shrink) and then migrate to estuarine and mangrove habitats where they grow by feeding on, at, or near the surface on insects, copepods, shrimp, and small fish. As they grow, they feed on larger foods, eventually preying on mullet, mollies, silversides, marine catfish, shrimp, crabs, and menhaden, among other fish.

Male tarpon can live around 30 years (maximum age observed was 43) and attain sizes up to around 100 pounds. Females live longer, approximately 50 years (oldest observed age 55), and can reach 300 pounds. Because we are, in this book, primarily talking about giant tarpon, those fish over 100 pounds, it is no accident that I, from time to time, refer to the fish as "she." New studies indicate we may have underestimated their life span and some fish exceed that by ten years or so. The all-tackle world record (additionally certified as the 80-pound-class record) for a giant tarpon is 286-pounds, 9-ounces caught by Max Domecq in Rubane, Guinea-Bissau, Africa, on March 20, 2003.

Atlantic tarpon have a wide range throughout the central Atlantic Ocean, and their "comfort zone" loosely corresponds to the range of the tropical and subtropical mangroves. In the western At-

lantic, tarpon are only caught with any regularity (though the catch numbers are only a sliver of catches farther south) as far north as Virginia's eastern shore, where anglers successfully target them in July and August. The bulk of the fish are caught south of Virginia to Bermuda and in the Gulf of Mexico. The Caribbean Sea has good stocks of tarpon, with fisheries in Brazil and Costa Rica, among other places. In the eastern Atlantic, tarpon occur most frequently along the west coast of Africa from Angola to Senegal. Genetic studies have shown that the populations in the western Atlantic intermix, but that the populations in Africa are more or less distinct from those that migrate along the coast of the United States.

Habitats

Tarpon are not as sensitive to freshwater intrusion as some fish. In fact, during the summer, they seek out brackish or pure freshwater environments. Boca Grande, Homosassa, and the Everglades all have a constant flow of fresh water entering the Gulf and are prime spots for tarpon. Because of this ability to live in a wide variety of habitats, and their ability to breathe air and live in water with low oxygen, juvenile tarpon can live in golf-course ponds, canals, and out-of-the-way places.

The range of temperature tolerance for adult tarpon is 62 to 96 degrees F. I'm not sure what their optimal temperature is, but in the early spring in Boca Grande we find the fish in 72- to 74-degree water, and studies have shown that during their offshore migrations tarpon tend to prefer the 78-degree isotherm. I think it is safe to assume that their ideal temperatures are in the middle of the 62 to 96 range, or 70 to 85 degrees, though the water being warm enough is more important than it being too warm. Cold water below 50 degrees F is lethal, and winter cold spells can kill tarpon that do not have access to deeper, warmer water.

The differences between tarpon fisheries are less significant than what they share. A flow of

Tarpon are road warriors, following the highways laid out by the contours and bars on the ocean's floor.

fresh water mixed with salt is one common denominator. Charlotte Harbor, the backdrop to the passes and beaches of Boca Grande, is fed by the Myakka and Peace rivers, which provide an increasing flow of fresh water as the rainy season intensifies in midsummer. As this continues, huge numbers of fish push east and stage up, feeding in the stained brackish waters of Charlotte Harbor. The same influx of freshwater intrusion is apparent in the backcountry of the Keys from the Everglades. The Homosassa flats are fed their fair share of sweet water from numerous tributaries such as

the Crystal River, Homosassa River, Chassahowitzka River, and Weeki Wachee Springs.

Food sources vary from one fishery to another
but abundance is the key to maintain a large population of breeding-size tarpon. Grass beds with
consistent water depths ranging from 5 to 8 feet
seemed to be preferred for backcountry habitats.
Areas located in moderate to strong tidal flow patterns are also a universal requirement. While
spawning habits still remain a mystery, the fish
need access to offshore locations.

Some of the other ingredients that make excellent fisheries, as much for fishermen as for the fish,
are access to both ocean and backcountry fishing
(which both Boca Grande and the Keys provide)

and white sand bottoms that make spotting and
sight-fishing to the tarpon easier. Water clarity is
also a factor—more for fishermen than the fish.
Water in the Keys is considerably clearer, making
it easier to see fish but much tougher to get them
to eat the fly.

Boca Grande and the Keys are relatively user-
friendly. Homosassa is not. Homosassa is by far the
most physically challenging tarpon fishery I've en-
countered. No backcountry islands or sandbars
offer anglers the option of tucking inside when it
gets windy. Outcroppings of jagged craters litter
the Gulf's floor, jutting upward like headstones
that mark the final resting places of more than a
few lower units that have been sheared off over

Tommy Locke and client searching for tarpon in Boca Grande, one of the world's greatest tarpon fisheries. JAY NICHOLS PHOTO

the years. The craggy crevices of these black rocks have a special knack for taking a viselike stranglehold on push-pole tips, shearing them off like toothpicks and launching even the most surefooted guides into the water. The only things tougher than the environment are the guides, and I respect their talent and rawhide mentality. Anything less won't work on these flats. Because of the challenging fishing conditions, you should hire a guide to be successful in Homosassa. I do, and I've been banging around those rock piles for a long time.

So what's the lure of this difficult fishery? During the first two weeks or so of May, anglers stand a chance of hooking up to a special kind of tarpon. Not only is the average size of Homosassa fish larger than those in Boca Grande or the Keys, but they look different. Unlike the more graceful, streamlined tarpon elsewhere in Florida, these fish are stocky with coal-black backs. These Homosassa black backs are meaner and more unpredictable than tarpon elsewhere. They arrive and leave when they're good and ready. Homosassa tarpon fishing isn't a numbers game, except when it comes to calculating weight.

As of 2008, twenty-nine world-record tarpon have been caught in Florida, and all of the major fly-fishing records have been caught in the Homosassa area, no doubt why it is considered a mecca for giant tarpon. In 1982, Billy Pate set a fly-fishing record on 16-pound tippet with a 188-pound tarpon caught off of Homosassa. Pate's 16-pound-tippet record was broken on May 13, 2003, with a 190-pound, 9-ounce tarpon caught by Tom Evans Jr. Evans was guided by Captain Al Doparik. On May 11, 2001, Jim Holland Jr., guided by Captain Steve Kirkpatrick, caught the first tarpon on fly over 200 pounds—a 202-pound, 8-ounce fish on 20-pound tippet.

Smaller numbers of tarpon also congregate in many other places throughout Florida and neighboring coastal states. These small pockets can provide great fishing as long as they are not overfished. Mosquito Lagoon, for instance, was too small and fragile to have the makings of a full-blown fishery like Boca Grande or the Keys, but we caught fair numbers of adult fish for years until word got out and more people started fishing it.

But the presence of tarpon is only one small part of actually being able to catch them. These fish swim in a complex environment of tides, weather, and changing seasons, and they respond to the habits and patterns of other things sharing the water—the baitfish they feed on, human pressure, and their predators such as sharks. Tarpon fishing is an ever-changing and complex game.

Migration and Spawning

The migration and spawning habits of tarpon still remain a mystery. While it is critical to understand these aspects for their conservation, understanding the factors that influence their travel patterns certainly won't hurt your fishing success rate. In Boca Grande, tarpon usually start showing up in numbers (like in many other fisheries, there are both resident and migratory populations) during the first to middle part of April. Perhaps because of swimming speed over the long journey, it's not unusual for smaller fish to arrive together. But it doesn't take long before strings of fish contain fish of varying sizes. Some have suggested that the fish appear in the nearshore waters at this time to feed before the spawning that occurs April through August in Florida, though some data suggests that they spawn as early as May and as late as October.

Though tarpon have not been observed spawning offshore, fertilized eggs have never been collected, and specific spawning sites have not been identified, scientists have attempted to deduce the spawning times and distances from the shore based on larvae collected offshore. In one instance, larvae three to six days old were collected and scientists were able to deduce that spawning took place in the Gulf of Mexico offshore of Florida at distances as far as 155 miles.

Biologists have identified that the presence of young larvae peaked with new and full moon phases, demonstrating that spawning occurs a week after each major moon phase. Scientists believe that they spawn at least four to five times each season. Though actual spawning has not been observed, many prespawning behaviors have been observed such as many smaller males bumping and accosting one large female repeatedly. Daisy-chaining (fish swimming in circles) is a common sight on the flats and may also be related to spawning.

As far as fishing is concerned, this means that the tarpon are migrating through the passes to the offshore areas shortly before each major moon phase, and they are returning shortly thereafter. And, since they are spawning multiple times each season, they are making this journey more than once. This combined with their daily movement for food and their movements associated with tides paints a very complicated picture—fish are coming and going and traveling here and there to eat and procreate, offering anglers with many chances to intercept them. Periods immediately

following postspawning activity can be superb fishing times because they feed heavily upon their return.

In addition to movements related to spawning and feeding, the Bonefish Research Project at the University of Miami and Bonefish and Tarpon Unlimited's (BTU) tagging efforts and satellite pop-up archival transmitters (PATs) are revealing some interesting facts about the travel habits of tarpon.

The PAT is designed to be towed by a tarpon for a preprogrammed time period, which may be up to two years, after which it automatically releases itself from the fish, floats to the surface, and transmits its recorded data to an orbiting satellite. These tags are approximately 6 inches long and 1 $1/2$ inches in diameter. Once a tarpon is caught with a rod and reel, they are attached to the tarpon high on the back behind the head. These tags are set to record temperature, water depth, and locations at various times during the day.

Based on data from the PATs and tagging, biologists have learned that tarpon cover a lot more

Daisy-chaining is probably pre-spawning behavior, though why they all of a sudden start circling is still a mystery. No matter the reason, it is an excellent opportunity to catch a fish.

ground than initially thought. In general, evidence suggests that tarpon will travel hundreds to thousands of miles in less than two months. Tarpon tagged off of North Carolina have been captured off Cuba's southern coast, and fish tagged off of Mexico have later been captured in Texas, Louisiana, and other Gulf states. Data retrieved from one PAT showed a 171-pound tarpon traveled 1,073 miles from Veracruz, Mexico, to Timbalier, Louisiana, over a 102-day period.

Tarpon along the U.S. Atlantic coasts and western Gulf of Mexico appear to make seasonal migrations, moving north in the spring and early summer and returning south in the fall and winter. But the extent to which populations, say those from Florida and those from the Caribbean, mix is not well understood.

The Future of the Fishery

When they are older, tarpon's primary predators are bull and hammerhead sharks and humans. Though they are only harvested for food or other commercial consumption in a few countries, angler mortality through improper catch-and-release or killing fish for the record books is a minor factor in the fish's mortality rates.

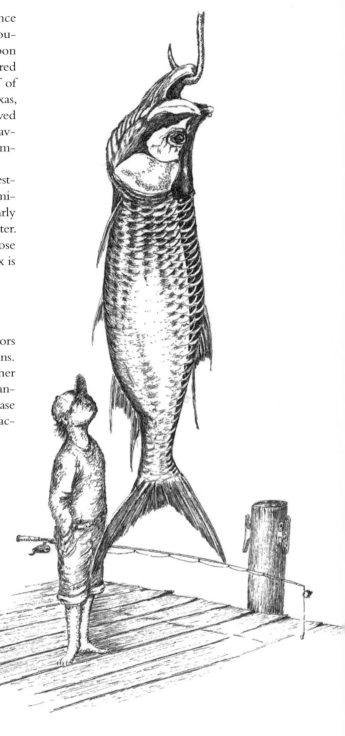

Fortunately, the classic photos of victorious fishermen posing next to tarpon hung by their jaws like fallen ironclad gladiators are a thing of the past.

Fortunately, the classic photos of victorious fishermen posing next to tarpon hung by their jaws like fallen ironclad gladiators are a thing of the past. But a word of caution is in order. It's easy to be judgmental when looking back at what anglers and hunters used to do. Just in my lifetime, practices that were once considered acceptable are not today.

When I was a boy, we perceived the inventory of wild game and fish to be bottomless. We toted every fish, regardless of size, to the cleaning table, filleted them, and froze them in waxed milk cartons. Far from feeling guilty, I felt as lucky and proud as those dudes with the bow ties, dress shirts, and Calcutta boat rods propped up next to the tarpon they just dragged out of Boca Grande Pass for nothing more than a smile and a photograph.

That felt right then, but it wouldn't now. I don't regret or apologize for any of it. The truth is, we couldn't be where we are today without scrambling down the road it took to get here. Looking back at where we've been gives us a clearer picture of how to assure the future of our tarpon population is safe and secure.

Even though killing fish is still part of the tarpon fly-fishing game, at least for some, we are killing a lot fewer of them. As of 1989 Florida anglers must obtain a tarpon tag to possess and deliberately kill them. If a tarpon is caught and immediately released, it has not come under possession and no tag is required. The permit costs $50 for each tarpon (limit two per day), and the anglers who purchase the tag agree to provide the Florida Marine Research Institute with information about the catch, including date and location of capture, the length and weight of the fish, and how many anglers were fishing. Guides who purchase tags can transfer them to their clients. According to Florida Fish and Wildlife Commission data, in 1993–1994 there were 357 permits issued and 84 tags used, and ten years later, in 2003–2004, there were 297 permits issues and 49 reported harvested—almost half as many killed fish.

The biological story of tarpon still has as many questions as answers, but thanks to the hard work of organizations like Bonefish and Tarpon Unlimited new data is coming down the pipe at a steady rate. One can only hope the result of all this will reveal more information to help us continue to enjoy the thrill of catching them as well as to protect this valuable resource.

CHAPTER THREE

Leaders and Connections

f you have never tarpon fished before, it might seem odd that I am starting out with a discussion of leaders rather than rods, reels, or flies. But, of all the components in the tackle box used to hook, fight, and land these brawlers, the leader is the weakest link in the chain and the part that receives the most attention from dedicated tarpon anglers.

Not only are you trying to subdue a fish that weighs many times the breaking strength of the leader—for instance, a 100-pound fish on 16-pound-test—but there is an inherent challenge of attaching pieces of monofilament of radically dissimilar sizes. It can be difficult to attach an 80- to 100-pound bite leader to a lightweight class tippet ranging from 20- to 6-pound-test so that the knot consistently tests out as close to 100 percent as possible.

I tie about 250 tarpon leaders each season, and tie them all to International Game Fish Association (IGFA) specifications for two important reasons. First, I always want to be prepared to catch a record fish, and not fishing with leaders tied to IGFA specifications would render the record in-

valid. Second, and perhaps more importantly, tying all of my leaders to strict specifications ensures consistency. Over time I have learned exactly how much pressure I can apply on a fish before breaking the leader. Even if you are not interested in playing by the IGFA's rules, you should still build and finish each leader the same way to be able to consistently measure the pressure you apply to every tarpon you fight.

Why is consistency important? You want to know what the breaking point of your leader is so that you can apply maximum pressure on the fish. If one day you are fishing 30-pound-test and the next day 20-pound, or if your class tippet is 15 inches one day and 24 inches the next, and you use different knots each time, there is no way to ensure you are applying maximum pressure. If all your knots are the same, and the lengths are equal every time, there is a way to know.

When I am pulling on a fish, I think about how to protect my leader: Is it over or under the pectoral fin? Is the fish hooked on the outside of her mouth or way inside? If I see the bite leader

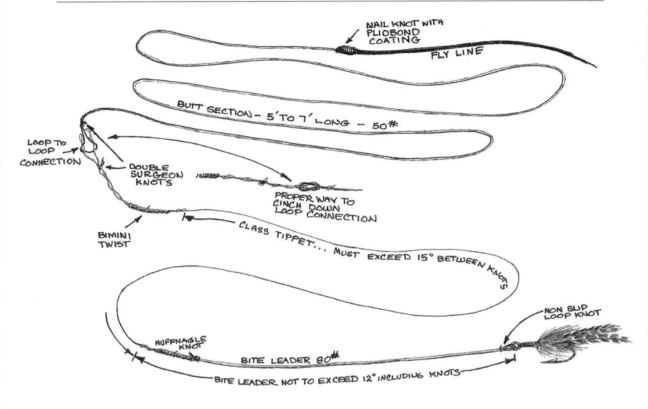

NAIL KNOT WITH PLIOBOND COATING

FLY LINE

BUTT SECTION – 5' TO 7' LONG – 50#

LOOP TO LOOP CONNECTION

DOUBLE SURGEON KNOTS

PROPER WAY TO CINCH DOWN LOOP CONNECTION

BIMINI TWIST

CLASS TIPPET... MUST EXCEED 15" BETWEEN KNOTS

NON SLIP LOOP KNOT

HUFFNAGLE KNOT

BITE LEADER 80#

BITE LEADER NOT TO EXCEED 12" INCLUDING KNOTS

The author's IGFA tarpon-leader system.

curling back under her lip, I know it is getting a lot of wear. The top of a tarpon's mouth on the inside is like sandpaper. On the outside, the bite leader is probably getting less wear. Late in the fight, all the stretch is gone from the leader and it might be chafed. With all the things that can weaken the leader through the fight, it is critical you start with the strongest leader possible.

I am going to describe the process of tying a tarpon leader that has worked well for me. Using the same knots for hundreds of tarpon leaders each season gives me an enormous amount of confidence, and it is critical to have confidence in your system. But, leaders and knots involve a lot of personal choices, and other anglers may prefer other methods. Once you start to believe your way is the only way, you stop learning, and I'd

change my system in a second if it stopped working for me.

Pick a series of time-tested knots and practice them until you can tie them in your sleep. I had the worst time learning to tie Bimini knots. Finally, I purchased a large spool of cheap line and kept it in the upper drawer of my desk. During lengthy phone calls, I practiced my Biminis until I got them right. If you, like me, have a hard time picking up knots from a book alone, an excellent instructional aid is Lefty Kreh's new book, *Fishing Knots* (Stackpole Books, 2007), which also includes a DVD.

Building the Leader

A tarpon leader has three parts: the butt section, class tippet, and bite leader (also called a shock leader). The class tippet and bite leaders are assembled and attached to flies and stored in a leader stretcher. When you need to attach or change flies, you loop-to-loop them to a straight piece of leader connected to the fly line, which is called the butt section. The butt section can vary in length depending on personal preferences and water conditions, and it stays on the fly line at all times, unless it needs to be changed because of wear and tear.

According to IGFA rules, the class tippet must be at least 15 inches long (measured inside connecting knots). The bite tippet can't be longer than 12 inches, measured from the hook eye to the single strand of the class tippet, and includes any knots used to connect the bite tippet to the class tippet. If they are not fishing IGFA leaders, many guides will use a fairly lengthy section of bite tippet (much longer than the 12 inches, say 2 feet) and just clip off the fly and tie another knot so they do not have to change the entire leader. To ensure their clients land the fish, they also may use 20-pound or higher class tippets.

When I tie my leaders, I tie the class tippet first and then attach the class tippet to the bite leader, which already is tied to the fly. The class tippet and bite tippet become an integral part of the fly. When

I change flies, I change everything to ensure consistency and to prevent shortening the 12-inch bite tippet. While I prefer to have all my flies prerigged, I often carry some leaders with a slightly longer bite section and leave those in my tackle bag in case I want to fish a fly that I didn't plan on using.

Knot tying is not a matter of speed. It's the quality that matters most. For this reason, I am meticulous when tying leaders. I've heard of people tying them in the dim light of a hotel room or in the boat (and sometimes I guess you have no choice), but I prefer to tie them all at home, in good light, with a setup that I have developed to make the process as simple and consistent as possible. I am such a stickler about my leaders that I don't even enjoy a cocktail when working on them. Many things go well with whiskey, such as music and playing pool, but leaders are best put together when you are.

Tying the Class Tippet

When I build a leader, the first thing that I do is build the class tippet. The tippet is called "class" tippet because of the different IGFA pound-test-class categories (6-, 8-, 10-, 12-, 16-, and 20-pound). A lot of the guides that I know fish 30- and 40-pound-test instead of the lighter tippet. While I can

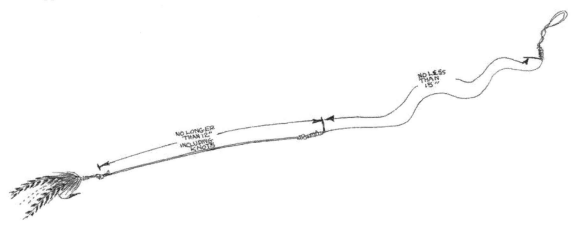

A tarpon leader consists of a butt section, class tippet, and bite leader. An IGFA class tippet must be at least 15 inches long, and the bite tippet cannot exceed 12 inches, including the knots.

understand the guide's motivation for this (get the client a tarpon), I think anything over 20–pound-test allows the angler to get away with poor techniques during the fight. A few guides don't allow their anglers to use anything over 20-pound. Every angler on Tommy Locke's skiff fishes 16-pound because he cares about teaching fish-fighting techniques. At the end of the day, the angler who catches a tarpon on an IGFA 16-pound-test leader can be proud that he battled the tarpon on a level playing field.

Beyond any threat of robbing the angler of the satisfaction of playing and landing a fish on lighter tippets, there is the very real threat of getting your fingers or toes caught in a loop of fly line as a 150-pound tarpon pulls off line. My grandkids are just starting to throw plugs at tarpon. The oldest is seven. When I tie on the plug, I slip a section of 8-pound between the line and the leader because I want to keep them and the outfit inside the boat.

The class tippet is really the critical part of the entire leader system because it is the weakest link. I tie most of mine about 17 inches long because I want to be over the IGFA 15–inch limit, and I like the extra little bit of stretch from the longer class tippet. Any longer and I find that the tippet can rub against the tarpon's body or get caught on the pectoral fin.

The goal when tying the class tippet is to make loops on both ends with Bimini twists and have the total length of the class tippet come out about the same each time. The Bimini on one end connects to the bite tippet with a Huffnagle (or other knot), and the second Bimini enables you to attach the class tippet to the leader butt with a loop-to-loop connection.

The Bimini twist is a great knot for this purpose for several reasons. First, it is a 100 percent knot, so you lose no strength by using it. Second, you increase the line's diameter by doubling it, which makes it easier to connect to the much larger bite tippet. The greater the disparity in diameter between lines, the more challenging it is to connect them. The third benefit of using a Bimini is that the twists in the line act as a bungee cord and provide more stretch and shock absorption than a single strand of monofilament. This extra stretch helps protect against any sudden jerks or surges, which are what most often cause the line to break. When you are in the last minutes of your fight and the fish is up close to the boat, you are often hanging on with only your butt section and the balance of the leader. The advantage of the forgiving stretch offered by the fly line is gone, and you need every little bit of help you can get to protect against a sudden head shake or surge from the fish.

With only twenty turns this cushion is not nearly as dramatic as a leader tied with a 50- or 100-turn Bimini, which is what I use at the top of the class tippet when fishing 6- or 8-pound-test. The reason that I do not use a 100-turn Bimini on the bottom is that the knot is very long and reduces the length of my bite leader. Remember, the 12 inches allowed by IGFA includes the knot tied to the class tippet.

I pull off a 3- to 4-foot strand of Rio monofilament or Mason hard nylon from the spool to ensure that I have plenty of line to work with. If the tag end is too short, it is hard to work with, and if it is too long, it is cumbersome to make the finish wraps.

Tie your first Bimini. The conventional way of tying a Bimini is to form a loop of line, insert your hand into the loop, and start wrapping. Because I prepare so many leaders each season, it quickly became clear to me that this method wasted time and was too hard on my wrist. After rigging twenty 100-turn Biminis for my 6-pound leaders, I would need medical attention. Instead, I make the turns with a battery-operated drill with an Allen wrench inserted in the chuck. Wrapping the bend of the wrench with tape protects the line.

Slightly offset the loop around the end of the Allen wrench. This will tug the hand holding the loop forward slightly with each revolution. Count

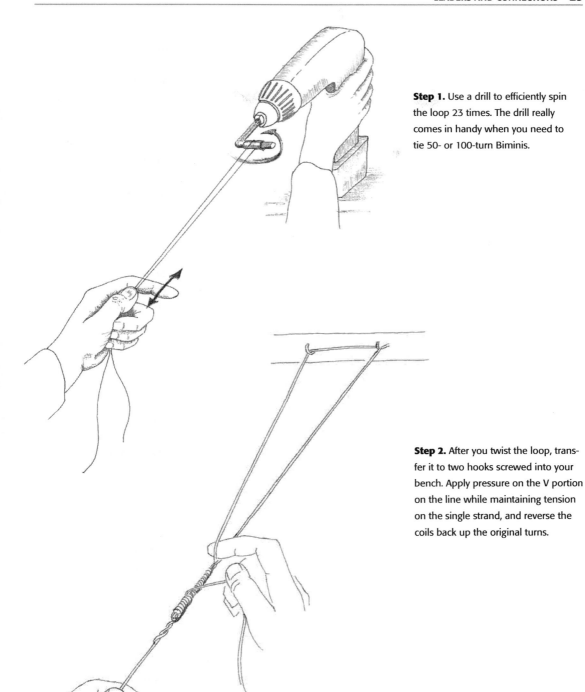

Step 1. Use a drill to efficiently spin the loop 23 times. The drill really comes in handy when you need to tie 50- or 100-turn Biminis.

Step 2. After you twist the loop, transfer it to two hooks screwed into your bench. Apply pressure on the V portion on the line while maintaining tension on the single strand, and reverse the coils back up the original turns.

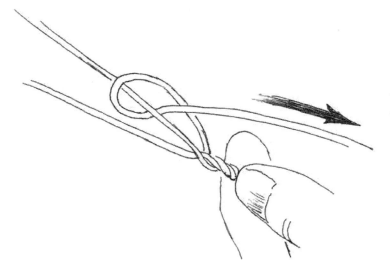

Step 3. Pinch the last few coils with your left thumb and forefinger, and tie a half-hitch on one leg of the V.

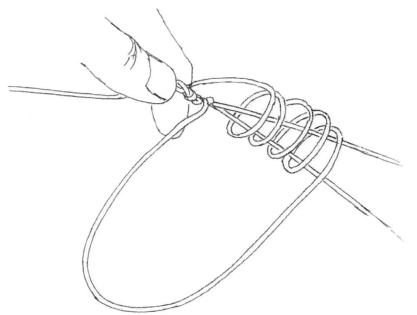

Step 4. Wrap five turns around both sides of the V.

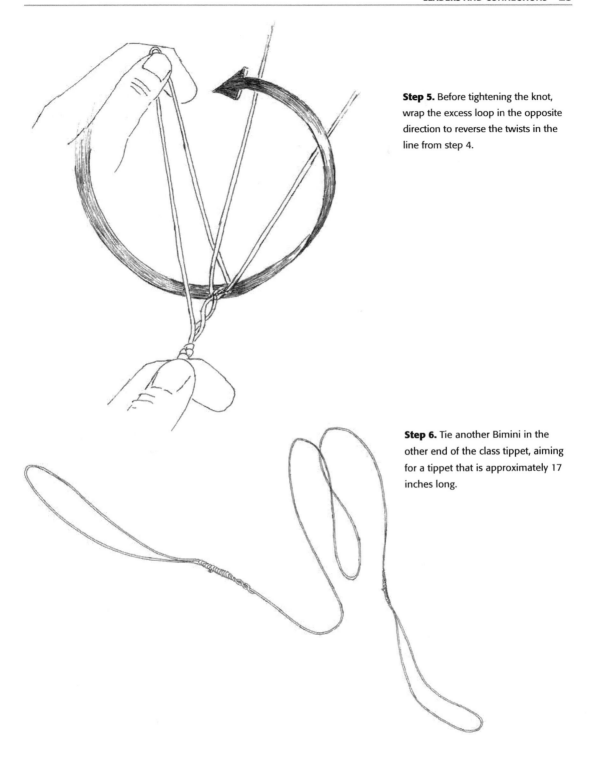

Step 5. Before tightening the knot, wrap the excess loop in the opposite direction to reverse the twists in the line from step 4.

Step 6. Tie another Bimini in the other end of the class tippet, aiming for a tippet that is approximately 17 inches long.

each tug to achieve the required number of wraps. With 16-pound, I like twenty-three revolutions. Not twenty-two and not twenty-four. It's not that twenty-three turns is better than one or two turns more or less, but it's the consistency from one leader to the next that matters most. I don't want one leader to have twenty-five wraps and the next to have twenty-two. We Floridians may have a hard time counting those hanging chads, but we've got the number of turns in a Bimini down to a science.

Once I spin twenty-three turns, I transfer the loop of the Bimini to two hooks screwed into the front edge of my fly-tying bench. I then apply pressure toward me on the V portion on the line while maintaining tension on the single strand, and reverse the coils back up the original turns. The coils should be angled slightly. I am careful to make sure the first few turns are not barreled against one another, causing a sharp turn that pinches against the single strand of line as they move back up the line. Once I have made a few loose wraps, I tighten the wraps. When I first started fishing with Tommy Locke, I noticed his leaders were tied this way, and Lefty Kreh would later confirm that the few open spiral turns make the knot stronger, even though they slightly increase the length of the Bimini.

Once I have reached the top of the knot, I pinch the last few coils with my left thumb and forefinger and tie a half-hitch on one leg of the V. As I snug the half-hitch in place, I am cautious not to over tighten the knot to the point it migh t crimp the single strand of line. I then wrap five turns around both sides of the V. Some folks put more. Before tightening the knot, I wrap the excess loop in the opposite direction to reverse the twists in the line from the five turns. Lefty showed this to me years ago, and it makes working the five half-hitches down to the single-leg half-hitch a real cinch. There is no chance of overlapping the coils this way.

As I begin the process of finishing these knots, I tend to increase the amount of pressure used to cinch the knot to its final resting place. For exam-

ple, I don't draw the knot quite as tight when making that first half-hitch around the single strand as I will around the doubled line for fear that too much pressure on the first half-hitch might crimp or bite into the line. This is much the same idea as keeping the initial turns of the Bimini loose before beginning the barrel rolls.

Though class tippets must be no shorter than 15 inches between the knots to meet IGFA standards, there is no maximum length restriction. To ensure my class tippets meet this standard I tie my class tippets about 17 inches long. After tying the first Bimini, measure 15 inches and make that the spot you pinch the line with your fingers to form the loop that will form the beginning of the second Bimini. Now you are confident the leader will be no shorter than 15 inches. After you have made the desired turns and the loop is in place over the half hoops on the table in front of you, simply spread the tag end of the line and the line to be the class tippet before finishing the knot. This will add a few inches to the single strand of the class tippet, making it over the required 15 inches.

After I tie the class tippet, I locate the end that has the longest loop (one always ends up slightly longer) and I hang it around my neck, always keeping the one with the longest loop on my right side so that I know where it is, and move on to the next step, which is to connect the fly to the bite leader.

Connecting Fly to Bite Leader

Before connecting the class tippet to the bite leader, I connect the heavy bite tippet to the fly so that I can use the hook to help tighten the Huffnagle, the knot used to attach the bite to the class tippet. I like an adjustable loop knot such as the Homer Rhodes or the Kreh Nonslip Loop. If the loop is too small, it not only restricts the fly's movement, but the leader can bind in the hook eye, locking the fly on an angle. I prefer a loop that is about 1/4 inch long. If the loop is too big, fish might detect it.

Though a loop provides better action for the fly, I don't think that attribute is all that important for tarpon. When I am feeding a fish, it is not my objective to get the fly to bounce or move around a lot. I want the tarpon fly to drag and pull straight. In this regard, I think many old-school anglers had it right by snelling the bite leader to the bare shank in the front of the fly, common with many of the Keys-style patterns. Snelling provides a straight pull, allowing the fly to track better in the water.

A loop knot is a better choice for reasons that have nothing to do with the fly's action. To understand this fully, we need to revisit the difficulty of setting a hook in a tarpon's bony mouth. Once the tarpon has taken the fly and turned, the hook may or may not find a place to begin to penetrate. This is not a friendly place for hook points. Unlike many other fish, there's not much meat or muscle exposed on the walls of a tarpon's mouth. But creases and crevices where the various components come together offer places for a correctly sharpened hook point to hang. A fly tied to the bite leader with a loop knot is more apt to do this because it's free to move around in the fish's mouth.

Connecting Class Tippet to Bite Leader

The bite leader's sole purpose is to provide abrasion resistance against the inside of a tarpon's mouth while you are fighting the fish. I use 80-pound Orvis Mirage fluorocarbon. The waters I typically fish are generally stained enough to get by with 80-pound, though in clear water (such as the Keys), you may have to use a lot less. Fluorocarbon straightens easily. Pull off what you need, pull the leader tight, and grip the line between your thumb and forefinger, rubbing back and forth several times. This heats the line up and straightens it. Storing the leaders in a stretcher keeps them that way.

Including all knots, the section of bite leader cannot exceed 12 inches by IGFA standards (from the point of the single strand of class tippet to the

hook eye). Sometimes, when the fish inhales the fly beyond the bite tippet, 12 inches is not enough. But those are the rules I elect to play by.

I am old school when it comes to connecting 16-pound-test to 80-pound-test fluorocarbon. A Huffnagle does the job just fine for me. The toughest part about tying this knot is the name. Measure up the bite leader from the hook eye 10 3/4 inches, and crimp the bite tippet 90 degrees with pliers. With the Bimini, the entire knot should come out to be about 11 3/4 inches long. The bite leader must not exceed 12 inches, and the 1/4 inch shortfall should be ample to allow for any stretch during a long fight.

Though the Huffnagle today is most often showed with a single overhand knot, I tie a double in the bite leader close to the 90-degree crimp in the line. The double tends to make the knot slightly bulkier than the single, but I have not found that it makes a difference to the fish, and it is the way that I learned it. Draw it together, but do not close it all the way, allowing the humps in the knot to form against the crimp in the leader.

Inspect your class tippet, and pick the shorter loop of the two. (The longer loop will make it easier to finish the top half of the leader.) Pinch the end of the shorter loop, and feed it through the two humps standing upright in the double half-hitch. Remember, the 16-pound class tippet is now doubled in size due to the Bimini. This gets the line diameter a little closer in diameter to the bite leader.

Place the hook in one of the half hoops mounted on the edge of your bench. Grip the tag end of the bite leader with a pair of pliers, slide the Bimini up against the half-hitches, and cinch the humps down nice and tight. Pull with your finger and with your pliers hand to close the double half-hitches and tuck the Bimini tight against the knot. Don't let up on the pressure. Pull with the pliers as you make a single half-hitch around the bite leader with the loop end of the Bimini. Some folks prefer numerous half-hitches behind the first one. This is optional. Make sure it's snug and keep it that way. Now make five turns around the bite leader and reverse your coils the same as you did for the Bimini. Cinch the knot down firmly and trim the excess.

One of the negatives of a Huffnagle is there is typically a bend in the finished knot where the Bimini and the half-hitches meet, which is caused by cinching the half-hitches down on the doubled

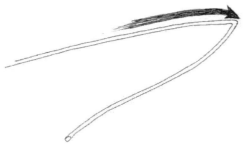

Step 1. Measure up the bite leader from the hook eye 10 3/4 inches, and crimp the bite tippet 90 degrees with pliers.

line. This does not weaken the line, but it should and can be minimized by keeping pressure on the knot with the pliers as you form the series of half-hitches with the Bimini loop. You can release pressure once these are completed and before you make the five or six finished turns.

I spray the knots with water through this process to make sure the line slides together easily, although Tommy Locke suggests that the finished knot cinches better without moistening because it heats the line up and bonds together better. Try both and see what works for you.

Connecting the class tippet to the bite leader with a Huffnagle makes for a bulky connection that is slightly out of line, but I use and trust this knot so much that I wouldn't switch unless I needed something better. Some anglers like an improved blood knot for connecting bite to class, and I have heard that the Slim Beauty knot also is a great alternative for the same purpose. It is used in the Keys, and I suspect its slimmer profile has

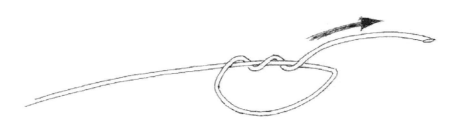

Step 2. Tie a double overhand knot in the bite leader. You can also tie a single.

Step 3. Pinch the end of the short loop, and feed through the two humps standing upright in the double half-hitch.

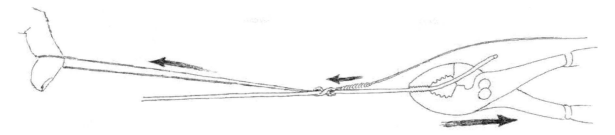

Step 4. Pull with your finger and with your pliers hand to close the double half-hitches and tuck the Bimini tight against the knot.

Step 5. Pull with the pliers as you make a single half-hitch around the bite leader with the loop end of the Bimini.

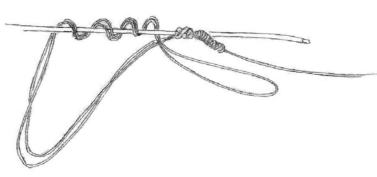

Step 6. Make five turns around the bite leader and reverse your coils the same as you did for the Bimini.

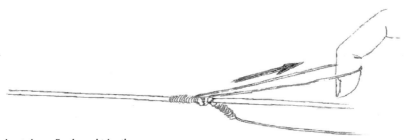

Step 7. Cinch the knot down firmly and trim the excess.

advantages over the Huffnagle in clear water. For great directions on tying this knot, see Lefty Kreh's *Fishing Knots.* If you are new to the sport, learn one knot or the other and stick with it so that you can tie them consistently. If you are a veteran and have been using one knot or the other with confidence, then I recommend sticking with what you have the most faith in. Faith in your leaders, and equipment in general, is a huge factor in the mental game of fishing for tarpon.

When tarpon break off—and they will—note where the leader broke. If it was inside or near the knot joining the tippet and the bite leader, the end of the broken line should be curled. If this happens on a recurring basis, something is wrong. Breaks should occur in the weakest link in the chain—somewhere in the single line of the class tippet.

Finishing the Class Tippet

The last step is to tie a double surgeon's knot in the loop so that there will be two loops to connect with the butt section. After you have tied the Huffnagle, remove the hook from the loop on your bench. With the drill, twist the longer loop approximately fifteen to twenty times (this number is not critically important). Then, put the loop around a nail. I have hammered a nail in my work bench and cut the head away. Then I covered the nail with shrink wrap tubing so the rough surface could not scar or damage the line. Pinch the area where the knot should be tied, allowing the twists in the line below this point to unravel. In the smooth area in the doubled line, tie a double surgeon's loop, making sure the loops remain the same length.

When you trim the tag ends, leave a 1/4-inch piece. These tag ends should be angled back toward the fly if everything was tied properly. I will cover this shortly when discussing storing rigged leaders.

Butt Section

A tarpon leader does not need to delicately turn over a fly like a bonefish leader or a freshwater trout leader. Its purpose is to keep the fly away from the fly line so the fish doesn't spook. The butt section, while part of the overall leader, is a straight piece of 7-foot 50-pound-test monofilament connected to the fly line. There is a loop at the end for attaching the prerigged fly and leader (bite tippet attached to class tippet). The overall length of my leaders is adjusted only by the length of the butt section. The overall length works out to be 9 1/2 feet to 12 1/2 feet depending on the butt section. I will vary the length of the butt section on different rods to accommodate different fishing applications. Spooky fish may require a longer leader. A longer leader also allows the fly to sink slightly more in the water column. A shorter leader can be delivered faster and tends to be more accurate. When I drop down and fish 6-pound-test, I use a 25- or 30-pound butt.

The butt section is more than just a link between the fly line and the class tippet. It also takes some abuse from the fish. If your entire leader is 10 or 11 feet and you are pulling straight back on a 6 1/2-foot fish, the butt section of the leader takes the brunt of the contact with the tail of the tarpon. When the butt section looks worn, I'll replace the worn piece with a blood knot, and then

Step 1. Twist the other loop fifteen to twenty times. Tie a surgeon's knot in the class tippet to form a double loop.

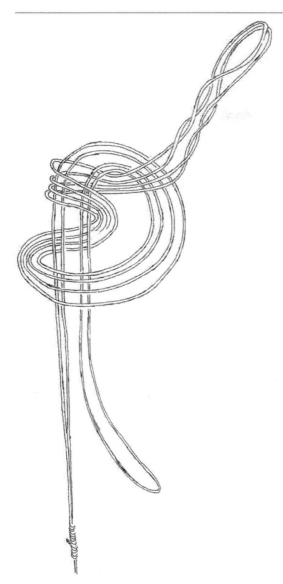

Step 2. Tie a double surgeon's loop knot in the loop.

make it easier for the knot to come through the first guide. At this point in the fight, the fish is only 10 or 11 feet away, and there is no room for forgiveness. There is no fly line to provide stretch and cushion. You have a tired leader and a lot of abrasion on your bite tippet, and you do not want anything to happen quickly.

Storing Leaders

I store my class tippets by coiling them and wrapping the end with the loop back inside the coils with three turns—every time. I change flies because one of three things happen. I have just caught a fish, I broke a fish off or it got off, or the fly that I have on isn't working. No matter what the reason, it seems like when I change flies, I am always in a big hurry. Using a consistent number of turns eliminates the thinking while unwrapping the looped end. I can do it quickly and without looking. Failing to unwind fully or unraveling too far can impart a half-hitch knot in the tippet when you stretch it out.

When storing leaders rigged to flies, coiled class tippets can pull apart or tangle as they jostle around in the boat. To help prevent this, years ago I started leaving an extra bit of tag end (1/4 inch) when trimming the lines from the loop connection. I call it my snaggle, and it helps capture the coils and lock them in place. The snaggle angles back toward the fly and does not pick up grass.

Leader stretchers are the most efficient way to store tarpon leaders already rigged to flies. While they do not stretch anything, they maintain the bite leader under slight pressure, keeping it straight and true. This is critical so the fly moves in a straight line as it's retrieved. In addition, a good stretcher also protects your class tippets and prevents wind from blowing the class tippets around and possibly tangling with one another.

I carry several stretchers with me in the skiff, including a nylon zippered case (manufactured by JW Outfitters). Some folks install stretchers under

nail-knot a new butt section on the fly line when I get back to the dock.

I attach the butt section to the fly line with a nail or needle knot coated with Pliobond. Other anglers like a loop-to-loop connection. When I am fighting a fish, I will lower and level the rod to

The "snaggle" prevents the coiled leader from unraveling.

the hatch lids of their skiffs, but I find it convenient to carry the stretcher inside the tackle room at the end of the day to reload with rigged flies. I also do not like to leave flies in the boat for too long because the hooks can rust. In my tackle room, I have a wall-mounted stretcher that I built to hold 280 rigged flies divided into pattern and color groups. This is my warehouse for rigged flies throughout the season.

Backing to Fly Line

For years I simply tied a Bimini in a single strand of 30-pound Dacron and connected it loop-to-loop with a loop whipped in the fly line. While this connection never failed, I noticed over time that the single strand loop cut deeply into the end of the loop in the fly line. Tommy Locke showed me a better way to make this connection. When you tie the Bimini in the backing, make the loop about 30 inches long. A few inches below the Bimini, double the loop and close it with a double surgeon's loop. Now instead of a single loop connecting the fly line to the backing, there are two. When closing the double surgeon's knot, be sure both loops are exactly the same size and don't interlace with one another. The two loops share the load when under pressure and do not cut into the fly line.

Rods, Rigged and Ready

I like to have several rods on board, rigged and ready with different length leaders. I carry at least three 12-weights. Two rods are rigged with floating lines: one with a 9¹/₂-foot leader and the other with a 12¹/₂-foot leader. I use the longer leader in clear water, and some anglers in the Keys fish even longer leaders. The extra length also allows the fly to sink slightly quicker than the shorter leader. The 9¹/₂-foot leader allows you to present your fly to a fish quickly and keeps it closer to the surface of the water. The third rod is rigged with a sinking-tip line, and I only use it in the backcountry when fish are deep.

CHAPTER FOUR

Flies

Fly patterns and colors are the top topics of conversation among tarpon anglers, perhaps because it is hard to nail down exactly why, when, and where fish seem to prefer certain patterns and colors one time, and then snub them the next. Or, why one pattern works extremely well one season and then bombs after that. When a tarpon fisherman finds something that works, it can become top-secret stuff. It's not uncommon for cagey anglers to remove their flies from the rods before returning to the dock so other anglers won't find out what they have been using. Maybe it is because we know so little about why patterns work that the good ones achieve almost supernatural status.

Adult tarpon eat a wide range of foods. They eat baitfish including threadfin herring (whitebait), mullet, pinfish, croakers, and glass minnows. They also feed on common ocean fare such as shrimp and crabs. They are also opportunistic feeders, seeking out locally important food sources such as crabs, palolo worms (in the Keys), mantis shrimp, and even sea horses. Certain fisheries have "events"—the two that come to mind are the hill

tide in Boca Grande Pass when tarpon gorge on pass crabs and the worm hatch in the Keys. You cannot forecast the timing and intensity of these events, but when they occur, word spreads like wildfire.

Palolo worms are the Keys megahatch that brings tarpon into a feeding frenzy. Each year in May and June in the Keys, 2- to 3-inch worms emerge from the coral rock in the ocean floor on falling tides in the late afternoon and evening and drift in the ocean current. Tarpon feed on them heavily.

Unlike the worm hatch, the hill tide in Boca Grande isn't really all that big of a deal for fly anglers. The effects of the hill tide are pretty much limited to the area around Boca Grande Pass and surrounding passes where pass crabs pour out with the spring tides of the new and full moons during May, June, and early July. The fish push eastward to the inside of the pass to a location known as the hill, feeding on the crabs being washed out. While some anglers attempt to catch tarpon on flies during the hill tide, the water is too deep to fight and land fish—especially with all the boats around. I

prefer to watch the show rather than joining in the fray. It's truly a sight to behold. Unlike the worm hatch in the Keys, the action is wall-to-wall tarpon busting crabs on the surface and wall-to-wall boats maneuvering for position. It's a hoot to stay off to the side during the hill tide and watch the action.

Despite these "hatches," day in and day out the flies that work best for me imitate baitfish or shrimp, crabs, and other critters. But I do not think that specific imitation is the most important attribute of a fly. For instance, I think it is more important that a fly be right for the water conditions. Larger flies with bolder profiles are often better choices in the backcountry or when fishing in low light. Smaller, sparser patterns are better choices when fishing on the beach. In the Florida Keys, where the water is crystal clear, effective fly patterns are often smaller and sparser. In Boca Grande, where we frequently have stained water caused by wind or runoff, the fish often take larger flies.

Size, Profile, and Color

Some days tarpon will eat anything you put in front of them. As Lefty says, "It's like rolling a wine bottle in a jail cell." But these days are few and far between, and choosing the right fly usually makes a big difference. Pattern size, bulk, and profile become more important in clear water or when the fish are pressured. Under these conditions, I go down in size.

If, after a good presentation, a fish shies away from my fly, I trim it with a pair of scissors that I keep handy in my pocket, changing the length, profile, or the bulk to make it look less obvious.

My goal is to be able to get the tarpon to see the fly, but not see it clearly enough to get a good look at it. Most often, I try to reduce the bulk (make it thinner) of the pattern, not its length, and then inspect it from the rear and from the bottom, which is the way the tarpon most often see it. A fisherman might pick up a fly, place it in his palm, and say, "Well, there it is. That looks really nice." But a tarpon does not see it that way. For starters, the tarpon sees the fly when it is wet and often backlit by the sun. On most good presentations, the tarpon is viewing the fly from the back and the bottom and from an angle. A 90-degree shot presents the fly to the fish broadside, but once the fish turns and follows, it is normally behind and below the fly. I feel that length is less important than the other two characteristics, in most circumstances. Threadfin herring, which tarpon eat routinely, are thin and come in all lengths.

Using a sparser amount of materials helps imitate the natural's translucence. But in darker water or low light, stronger, bolder colors like red and purple or black and purple provide a prominent silhouette that is more effective. Once I am convinced that I have done everything I can do to the fly to make it look right, I switch colors.

In general, I fish light-colored flies in clear water and dark-colored flies in dirty water. With my baitfish patterns, I like to carry two different patterns with different color combinations in both light and dark tones, which gives me a chance to change flies within each of the general categories of light or dark. I have a yellow/white and green/white Enrico Puglisi baitfish pattern for sunny days and clear water (generally when I am fishing the ocean side) and a black and purple and red and purple for backcountry fishing early in the morning when the light is low or when runoff clouds up the water later in the season. Brown also works well at this time.

Clear water, typical in the Keys, might be pretty to look at, but it's not helpful when feeding fish. At least in these conditions, it is easy to tell the difference between a positive response to a particular color or a flat-out refusal, which calls for an immediate fly change. As a rule, I will change colors before I switch to a different pattern.

When I was a boy my dad would leave me in a turkey blind before first light. His parting instructions were always the same: "Son, if the turkeys are getting bigger that means they're coming your way. Don't change anything! If they're getting smaller, they're going the other way, and do whatever you want!" In many ways, I think this also captures the essence of picking the right color or pattern of a fly. If you plop the wrong fly in a tarpon's face, it will get smaller fast. Change. If the fish gets bigger as you work the fly, you are on the right track. If someone tells you he knows more about color selection, then he's got more crap than a Christmas turkey.

The Patterns

I typically only use three different patterns in my home waters of Boca Grande: an Enrico Puglisi (EP) baitfish pattern, the Mouse, and a Cockroach. Though the tarpon eat a lot more foods than are represented by the patterns that I fish, I like to simplify my system. I am reluctant to add new flies

to my kit if the ones I already use are still working. Because I always am prepared with at least a dozen of each fly pattern, and four different color combinations, adding a new one adds up to forty-eight more flies that I have to rig and carry. Adopting a new fly pattern for the lineup and learning it's not effective is a lot like adopting a pet turtle. It's a lot of work with nothing gained in return. If I just fished a 3-foot bite leader and wasn't concerned about consistency or IGFA standards, I might carry a broader selection of flies, because I could just clip off one that was not working and experiment more.

To be sure, once the patterns that I am currently using have been thrown at enough fish by enough people, they'll stop being effective. But until I have to change, I'm slow to do it—not only from a warehousing and stock perspective, but because it takes a long time to become used to the behavior of each fly and how to effectively fish it under a range of conditions. The fewer things that I have to remember, the better I am able to perform. A dozen different flies would be too much for me to stay up with. Shoot, at the ATM the other day, I forgot my PIN and stood there like a zombie for ten minutes.

Simplifying my fly selection not only cuts down on rigging and decision making, it allows me to become keenly aware of the tiny nuances unique to each pattern, which I could not do if I fished twice as many patterns. Knowing how individual flies cast in the wind, land on the water's surface, or sink can make all the difference. The way the fly moves, sinks, and suspends in the water all make a difference. For instance, you can cast a slow-sinking EP baitfish much farther in front of a fish when you lead it, and the fly will still be in the strike zone when the fish meets it. Traditional Keys-style flies such as the Cockroach sink faster, so you can't lead a fish too far or the fly will sink out of view.

The flies that I use in my home waters of Boca Grande are also ones that I would feel comfortable using in Homosassa, but they may not be the best choices for every angler. For most folks, fly selection is an evolution of trial and error built around individual fishing tactics and habits—and having, for whatever reason, confidence in the pattern. Once I have confidence in a pattern, I use it regularly. The only time I'll stray from it is when nothing is working, which is normally when fish aren't feeding. And when the fish aren't feeding, it's hard to find any fly pattern that works consistently enough to inspire confidence.

EP Baitfish

Enrico Puglisi's baitfish patterns, like the Clouser Minnow or Lefty's Deceiver, represent a basic style of tying using EP Fibers, a synthetic material that comes in a wide range of colors, and featuring prominent eyes. This is my primary baitfish imitation. You can tie or buy many different color combinations, depending on water conditions, bait you are trying to match, and the tarpon's "mood" that day. I carry this fly in yellow and white, green and white, red and purple, black and purple, and brown. In general, I like to fish light or pastel colors for clear water and darker colors in cloudy or poor light conditions and murky water where I can't see the bottom. I fish these $3^1/2$- to 4-inch flies on #3/0 Gamakatsu hooks.

EP Fibers shed water easily, making this fly light, easy to cast, and silent when it hits the water. This may not be an important factor if you lead the fish far enough in choppy water, but you will not always have the time or proper angle for this. A soft landing is a must for laid-up fish. Sometimes, the fly doesn't sink right away, especially with commercially tied versions that tend to be a little heavier dressed than they need to be. You can help the fly sink by tugging it under or trimming it until it sinks. Trimming is best because tugging is an added step, and the last thing you need is another thing to do. Some anglers like the fact that it rests on the surface and the slight pull lets it start to go under. I don't, but you should experiment and see for yourself.

EP Baitfish.

Tied on the lighter hook, this fly sinks so slowly that it appears to just hang in the water, which is ideal for leading a fish. When you feed a tarpon, you want her to intercept the fly. If the pattern sinks too quickly, you have to time your cast too close to the fish to prevent it from sinking below the fish and out of that magic 2-foot cube in front of her face. I fish these flies with long, steady strips to get the fish's attention, sometimes increasing the speed and cadence to inspire a take.

A tarpon is built to eat up, and when you watch a fish getting ready to take a fly, she spreads out her pectoral fins like air brakes on full blast, trying desperately to stop her forward motion. Just like a vehicle, the rear rises up, the nose drops down, and the fish tries with everything she's got to stop her forward motion and get below the fly.

The EP baitfish has some negatives. Once it has been used a bit, the fibers twist together and the fly loses its shape and translucence. It also fouls a lot and you must check it carefully after each cast, especially backhanded ones. I keep a toothbrush handy to comb out the fibers when this occurs, finding that a comb rips out too many fibers.

The Mouse

The Mouse falls into what I call the critter category, looking a little bit like a shrimp, crab, or other food a tarpon might encounter. With its heavy front end and wiggly tail, this pattern is reminiscent of the currently popular Tarpon Toad.

I am not sure exactly what it "imitates," but tarpon are opportunistic feeders and eat a wide variety of foods. For instance, in July thousands of sea horses appear off the beach, and the tarpon feed on them, sipping sea horses one after the other. If you throw a Mouse into that melee, it will generally get eaten. In general this fly fishes best with short, subtle strips.

My favorite colors are brown and olive. With its bulky profile, this fly is a good choice for the backcountry or when runoff in the rainy season stains the water. Regardless of color, rabbit strips have too bold of an outline in clear water, so I usually do

The Mouse.

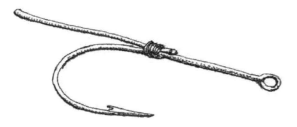

Step 1. Add a monofilament extension.

not use it when fishing the beach except when the water becomes cloudy from storms or rain runoff. I prefer the Mouse tied with a #3/0 Mustad 34007. The entire length should be less than 4 inches, and you can easily shorten it by trimming the rabbit-strip tail. Bead-chain eyes are an option but unnecessary for most fishing conditions.

Many years ago, Charlie Madden told me about the Mouse, and he was introduced to it by Captain Richard Keating of the Keys, who credits Randy Brown with inventing it some twenty-plus

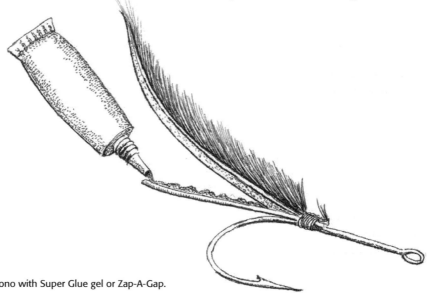

Step 2. Coat the mono with Super Glue gel or Zap-A-Gap.

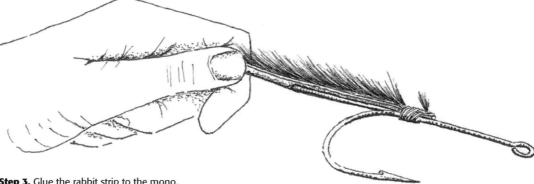

Step 3. Glue the rabbit strip to the mono.

years ago. Heaven only knows how many tarpon Richard has revived as a result of this one fly, and I thank him for allowing me to share it with you. If you want to know more about how to fish it, book Richard Keating for a few days—if he isn't booked solid.

Instead of saddle hackles, which the original recipe calls for, I prefer rabbit strips. To prevent them from fouling, my good friend David Olson showed me how to tie the rabbit strip to a short section of 80-pound monofilament extending from the hook shank. Later, I found that a bead of Super Glue gel run along the top of the mono holds the strip in place and is faster than lashing it with thread. If the mono is only long enough to keep the tail from fouling, about a shank-length beyond the bend, the rabbit strip still moves well in the water.

I have always been partial to grizzly hackles on Keys-style tarpon flies because of the contrast between the black and white bars. In an effort to add this same contrast to the Mouse, I started tying small pinches of black deer hair between each change of color. For example, I tip the nose of brown flies with a pinch of red deer hair and I use bright orange with the olive. This isn't so much for the fish as it is for me. On occasion, it enables me to see the fly more easily and evaluate its position relative to the approaching fish. Directly behind the nose color I add a small collar of black deer hair before tying in the brown or olive hair.

A few years ago I tied a rendition of this fly for my annual Homosassa trip with longtime friend and guide, Tommy Locke. Instead of the normal drab-olive deer hair, I used alternating bands of orange and black and nicknamed it the Tiger Mouse. I finally invented something! Our first day on the water, it took Tommy less than two seconds to pick up on the change I'd made: "What the heck is that?" As I dangled my prize tauntingly from the bite leader and smugly told him the new fly's name, he stretched out his hand. "Let me see that thing," he said.

As Tommy inspected the fly, I thought I would have a little fun with him. "Last night I made the mistake of leaving this thing zipped up in the stretcher with all the normal ones, and when I opened the case up this morning, he was the only one in there . . . along with some scraps of mono."

Tommy laughed aloud, "Oh really? What do you reckon happened to the others?"

I never broke stride: "Tiger mouse ate 'em. Guess he's not fond of leader material!"

Within the hour, a black-backed tarpon inhaled the fly well into the class tippet.

"Damn shame," announced Tommy from the platform.

I laughed aloud. "I'll say. That Tiger Mouse will eat that poor tarpon from the inside out in less than thirty minutes!"

The Cockroach

The Keys-style fly and its cousins have been responsible for more tarpon being pulled to the boat than any other pattern. Though I don't use it as often as the other flies, I rely on it for fishing in clear water or when I have exhausted my other options.

The Cockroach.

I keep a few small, buff-colored Cockroaches (#2/0 and #3/0 hooks, 2 to 2 1/2 inches) on the boat. I like to think of these patterns as small crabs or other ocean critters being swept along the tide, and I strip them very slowly.

From the Masters

When in an unfamiliar fishery, it pays to seek advice from the local experts. For instance, if I was going to the Keys, I'd call Sandy Moret of Florida Keys Outfitters in Islamorada to find out what the fish are chewing. In response to my question regarding his favorite fly for the Keys, Moret quipped, "As a fly-shop owner, my favorite flies are always the most expensive ones!" On a serious note, Sandy explained that for the two different fisheries in the Keys, the ocean side and the back-country, you need two different fly selections. On the ocean side he suggests flies that appear shrimpy or crabby; in the backcountry, baitfish patterns. He still regularly uses typical Keys-style flies.

Regarding Keys ocean-side fish, Moret has this to say: "They can be tough to feed. I change color or fly patterns once a good presentation has been made and refused inside that magic zone. It's a little like being at a cocktail party, and the girl walks up with a tray of meatballs and you pass. A short time later she returns with a tray of shrimp, and without thinking, you reach out and grab one." That's a terrific analogy for feeding clear-water tarpon.

When asked about his "go-to" fly, Flip Pallot responded, "Things have changed over the years. Tarpon have become manipulated by anglers presenting flies from the same points and ambush locations season after season. As a result, flies and hook sizes have continued to reduce in size. However, more important than pattern or color, anglers need to understand that fish have an area of awareness, the zone in which they are keenly aware of things that go on around them. I'm not

presumptuous enough to think I can deliver a fly inside that zone without it being viewed by the fish as a trespasser.

"There is a mental process I go through before presenting any fly to a fish. I can do it quickly given the years I've spent on the water. My objective is to have the fish enter or move into the area of awareness where I have placed the fly or have my offering delivered to the fish's zone by way of current or tidal movement. From that point, a fly that makes sense and is driven toward the fish like food by the angler will get eaten more times than not.

"I prefer flies tied to smaller hooks like Keys-style flies and Lefty's Deceivers. Smaller flies can remain inside the area of awareness longer without alerting fish and are more forgiving to mistakes due to their less obtrusive size."

When asked about fly selection for tarpon, Lefty Kreh's response was much the same as Flip's. His advice on patterns was precluded by counsel regarding proper presentation. Only then did he say that he prefers a "Lefty's Deceiver dressed in light colors" for clear water, and "a dark colored Lefty's Deceiver" for cloudy water or low light. When I asked about his favorite tarpon hook, he responded, "The Mustad 34007 SS has been and still is my first choice when it comes to tarpon."

These masters in the sport, Sandy, Flip, and Lefty, may vary slightly on their personal choice of patterns or colors, but each said essentially the same thing when asked about fly selection—pattern and color are secondary to presentation. No fly can make up for a bad delivery.

Once you've tied on a fly and made ready to introduce it to a tarpon, remember that you'll never get a second chance to make a first impression. Most of us have sat in a banquet room listening to the eloquent introduction of a guest speaker waiting to take the stage. In most cases, the speaker carefully selected the style, fit, and colors of his suit, tie, shirt, socks, and shoes. His clothing and

No fly pattern can overcome a poor presentation. If you want to hook up, you have to put the fly in the zone and work it in a believable way. MARK HATTER PHOTO

overall appearance make sense for the environment. Imagine the speaker appears looking like he stepped out of *GQ,* but then trips headfirst over the microphone cord and slides unconscious across the stage. There's not much his carefully selected attire can do at that point.

A Convenient Snack

It's normal for optimistic anglers to assume all tarpon are starving emaciated creatures waiting for you to plop something in front of them that will give them the substance to go on living. Nothing could be further from the truth. A 3-inch baitfish is not a full-course meal to an adult tarpon. It is a convenient snack and nothing more. The fly must catch the fish's interest and be *easy* for the fish to

eat. Only once have I seen a large tarpon swim past a fly, turn around, swim back, and eat it. It just doesn't make sense for that 100-pound fish to swim that far out of her way to chase a 3-inch fly, eat it, and then rejoin the string. So it has to be convenient and appealing, exactly the way Sandy Moret described it.

Sometimes I think a tarpon takes a well-placed fly just as an instinctive response. And yet, I have watched a fish take a long, hard look at the fly and then turn it down. I've seen them swim up and vibrate their bottom jaw against the tail of a fly like they have taste buds there and pull away. As a rule, when I see a tarpon get behind a fly and spend that much time looking at it, it is not going to get eaten. If it follows the fly 5 or 6 feet, it is getting too good a look and will most certainly pass it by.

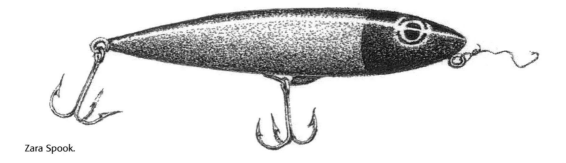

Zara Spook.

Standing Out in a Crowd

Matching size and shape of the predominate naturals works, but it may pay to make the fly look a little different from the real thing. A perfectly tied replica of a baitfish, worked in precise unison with the others, can get lost in the shuffle. You can make a fly stand out by its design or the action with which you fish it. For example, one of the most successful topwater plugs ever is the Zara Spook. "Walking the dog" can produce heart-stopping surface action by imitating an injured baitfish. Obviously this is not normal behavior for baitfish, but since it looks and sounds different, it attracts strikes. This is worth considering when selecting and fishing flies.

Conditioning

Even if the name of the fly is the Last Supper, if it's tossed in front of enough fish, enough times, by enough anglers, fish will eventually learn to reject it. And, this negative response can actually be passed down to future generations of that species within a fishery. For instance, twenty years ago in Mosquito Lagoon, local redfish would attack a quarter-ounce gold Johnson spoon. These spoons were so deadly, every angler used them. But, after awhile they were not as effective, and it got to the point where throwing one of those things in front of a red would actually spook them.

Today, the redfish in Mosquito Lagoon are many generations removed from the fish of the mid-1980s, but they still react negatively to this spoon, even though they have never seen one. This is common in many fisheries and I suspect more evident when dealing with fish with longer life spans such as redfish or tarpon, but I don't know this to be a fact. Lefty and I have discussed this many times, and he had noticed the same thing with fish like smallmouth bass and other species. It only goes to prove we are only seeing a part of the big picture.

Hooks

Someone once said that successfully hooking a tarpon is like dangling a fly inside a metal bucket and trying to get it to stick. Although it is not quite that difficult, tarpon are harder to hook than most fish because of their bony mouths.

A tarpon fly is only as good as the hook on which it is tied. The hook is the business end of the fly, and if it cannot penetrate the tarpon's hard mouth, you are out of business—no matter how much the fish like the fly. One of the best things that you can do to ensure solid hookups is to fish with sharp hooks. Some of the presharpened hooks on the market are fine. Some are not. A hook point that can't be sharpened after it gets dull renders the fly and the leader it's tied to useless.

The Mustad 34007 SS is my favorite tarpon hook. Though it is not factory sharpened, it is very

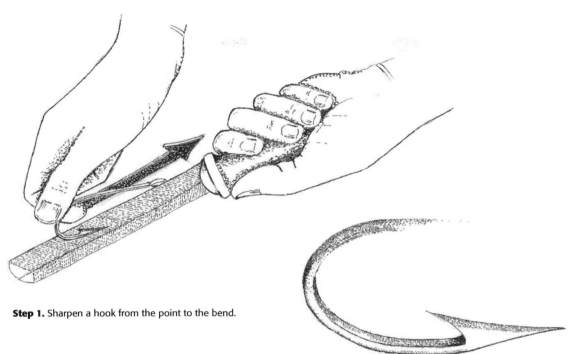

Step 1. Sharpen a hook from the point to the bend.

Step 2. A properly sharpened hook should stick in your nail.

strong and can be sharpened many times. I have only heard of one case where a 34007 SS broke during a tarpon fight, and that could have been because the file scarred the hook shank while sharpening it. It's easy to do if the file comes into the hook at too sharp of an angle.

Another dependable hook is the Gamakatsu SC 15, which is made from light wire and penetrates a tarpon's mouth better than thicker-wire hooks. Also, flies tied on this light-wire hook ride higher in the water column. The SC 15 can be resharpened easily with a file, and I sharpen the factory points a tad before using them.

I have not experimented with some of the newer hooks on the market because these two hooks have been so successful for me. I am open to most alternate options providing they are constructed from thin wire, can be resharpened easily, and are not circle hooks.

While circle hooks work well for live-bait anglers and deep-jigging enthusiasts, they are not a good choice for fly fishing. Effectively driving the

hook point of a fly deep in the bony mouth of a tarpon is a process that has been developed and passed down over time by pioneers such as Joe Brooks, Lefty Kreh, and Stu Apte.

When I hear people talk about how circle hooks are an improvement in fly fishing for tarpon, I think of the time that I took a trip to Bass Pro Shops with Flip Pallot to buy some new hunting boots. We tried on every pair they had, and we finally stumbled across a pair of the most comfortable boots either of us had seen. I grabbed a box, and on the way to the cashier, I noticed Flip was carrying two boxes. I couldn't help but ask, "Did you buy two pair?" Flip nodded, "Yep. Seems like a good idea to do so before they try to improve them!"

Like those boots, conventional hooks and hook-setting techniques do not need tweaking or

The barb on the hook prevents it from penetrating easily.

Partially pinch the barb with a pair of pliers. The hook will not back out during a fight.

improvement. Mastering the art of hook-setting takes time and dedication. A circle hook isn't a short cut or substitute for this hard work.

Anglers disagree about whether pinching the barb is a good idea, but I pinch the barb partially closed on the 34007 SS before using it. I think this allows greater penetration and makes the hook a lot easier to remove if you accidentally get it stuck in you. The hook doesn't back out during the fight.

Flip Pallot told me that following the countless tournaments in the Keys, he, Al Pflueger, and others would sneak in the cold storage room and experiment with different hooks and hook-setting techniques on the dead tarpon sprawled on the sawdust-ridden floor. This kind of dedication and desire to pull away the covers on our sport and find real answers is virtually nonexistent nowadays and exemplifies the passion that lives deep in the soul of all anglers who want to improve their skill as fly fishers for these magnificent fish. This is the length and breadth of the wake you and I follow today.

CHAPTER FIVE

Skiffs

As Lefty Kreh writes in *Fly Fishing in Salt Water,* the boat gets you to where you want to go, and it also becomes a platform on which you cast. How you set up in relation to the current, wind, and sun, and your angle to the approaching fish, can make or break any presentation. Tide levels and flow, and direction of the sun, wind, and sea conditions call for constant decisions regarding repositioning the skiff. Going even beyond that, a boat also becomes a critical tool when fighting large fish. At times, you can "dead-boat" (not pull anchor) smaller fish up to 100 pounds, but once you pull anchor and start to follow a larger fish, the boat (and the person handling it) becomes an integral part of fighting and landing it.

Boats are more than vehicles or tools. They have a certain magic to them. If I had to fish every day with a guide who ran the boat, I'd miss a large percentage of what I love about this sport. A half-hour ride in a skiff is much shorter than a half-hour ride in a truck. I'll never get tired of it.

My love affair with boats started with wood skiffs. Most kids experience their first taste of freedom with bicycles or a trip to the movies with

their buddies; mine came with the rental boats bobbing gunnel to gunnel in the slips at Stanford's in Englewood. My father would rent one for me along with a small kicker and turn me loose—shrimp in the baitwell built into the middle seat, a spinning rod, and a full tank of gas. My first taste of freedom came during those carefree summer days banging around the mangroves, and into every sandbar in the bay. As Alan Jackson sings, "You can't beat the way an old wood boat rides."

When, in 2001, I decided to build my own wood skiff, I went to see Bud Dewees. Dewees, owner and operator of LeFiles fish camp on Mosquito Lagoon, was a master wood-skiff builder, and many of his boats still run in the lagoon today. For the most part, they were working boats for the commercial-fishing community and while they were pleasing to the eye, they were far from the pretty mahogany skiffs coated with eight coats of varnish. I got to the point where I could spot one of his flat-bottom skiffs working in the lagoon a mile away. They had a proud bow gradually and gracefully falling away toward a low transom. The last boat he built that I recall seeing was a stand-up

row skiff tied in a slip at the dock. The oars were resting on stanchions or pillars in the place where the center seat would normally be, and the considerable amount of rocker in the center belly of the skiff caused the transom to sit almost as high above the waterline as the bow. I'm sure it spun on a dime.

Bud was also as gruff and tough as they came. When I was in high school, Bud had a handful of small travel trailers littered about the camp. One weekend a friend and I rented one. I recall trying to light the gas stove. There might have been a beer or two involved in the process, but in my defense, I had never even seen a gas stove. I turned on the gas, only to realize I had no matches. I walked the hundred yards or so to Bud's office and returned to the tiny trailer with my matches. The gas was still on when I lit one, and the explosion blew me out the door. Other than some serious damage to my eyebrows and pride, I was fine. The trailer didn't fare as well, and from that day on, Bud nicknamed me "dumb-ass."

Thirty-five years later, I sat on Bud's back porch at the fish camp watching his shaky hands sketch out the lines of a tiller skiff. I was finally going to build one myself. Bud was dying of throat cancer and was sick from chemotherapy.

"You want her to be light," his once strong voice whispered. "Use quarter-inch royal Douglas-fir on the sides and half-inch on the bottom." Bud threw up in a bucket next to the folding chair, and then continued: "Use a butt joint on the bottom and add no more than five inches of dead rise to the bow."

I made notes. By the time he finished his instructions, I had emptied the bucket many times. Bud got up, and I followed him a short distance to a metal shed near the edge of the water. We rummaged through sheets of dusty wood leaning against the wall. Bud didn't want the money I gave him but lacked the strength to put up much of a fight. Nodding to the stack of Douglas-fir in the bed of my truck, Bud told me: "Your boat's in that

During the time that we were making our trips to Jack Stanford's place in Englewood, Dad built a mahogany boat, without power tools, that he named the Miss "B." She was a thing of beauty. I cut my teeth driving that boat, until the transom rotted out it—typical of all wooden skiffs.

wood *Bill,* you'll have to hunt for it." I wasn't "dumb-ass" anymore.

It took eight weeks to build the skiff. Bud died in seven. I sure do wish he could have seen it.

The wood skiff is a great little boat for laid-up tarpon. I fish it partly out of nostalgia and maybe in

hopes Bud might get a glimpse of it, but most of all I fish it because it's fun. It is also extremely effective—light enough to pole all day and it spins on a dime. When I am fishing alone, I'll pole it from the bow, and it skims along on the water like a dinner plate. Because it also draws less water than my tarpon skiff, it's perfect for fishing way up in those nice little pockets in the creeks where the snook hold on an outgoing tide. To get to those spots, you may have to run a mile through 4 or 5 inches of water. It may be my imagination, but I think I've seen dust clouds rolling up from under the transom.

My main tarpon skiff is made from high-tech materials instead of wood, but there is magic in it, too. I customized a Hell's Bay Marquesa hull, which is well suited for the waters in Boca Grande, to suit my needs, which are primarily to develop a setup and a system to effectively fish for tarpon alone. Honest, it's not that folks don't want to go with me. I really prefer it that way.

I first got acquainted with Hell's Bay Boat-works when friends Flip Pallot and Hal Chittum, the two builders who started the company, used to test and fish some of the prototype boats near my house in Mosquito Lagoon. I learned a lot about them through their knowledge and their ability to design boats. I am not a boat-design aficionado. I've owned a lot of bad boats and a few good ones, which has taught me something. But guys like Flip Pallot, Hal Chittum, Tom Gordon, and Bob Hughes are the true talents. Scott Peterson, owner of Hell's Bay Boatworks, is on the cutting edge of some very exciting designs. Me, I just tinker.

When I started thinking about ways to make my boat easier to fish out of alone, I knew I wanted a raised helm. I was used to operating boats while standing up from my tiller-boat days, and after that, I never wanted to sit down and drive again. Standing afforded much better visibility, and the raised helm keeps me and my sunglasses dry. I was always aloft when running airboats with Pallot, and when I drove my tiller skiffs I stood on

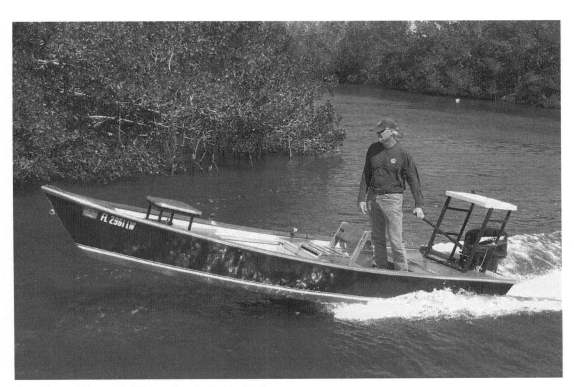

The author and his wood skiff. Boca Grande, Florida, 2008. SHANNON BROUILETTE PHOTO

Top view of the skiff. SHANNON BROUILETTE PHOTO

Raised console of the author's Hell's Bay skiff. Motorcycle struts provide support during long runs. SHANNON BROUILETTE PHOTO

the rear deck. I was not the first to come up with this idea on a tarpon skiff. I first saw it on guide Ronnie Richards's boats on the Homosassa flats. The console positioned far aft in the boat facilitates the best ride and free space in the cockpit, and the angled support struts for the raised helm make a perfect backrest for a passenger seat mounted on the lid of the built-in cooler. Initially the front edge of the poling platform served as a leaning post; however, a year or so later I added the bench seat to make long runs more comfortable. I installed motorcycle foot struts for my feet so that I can use my legs to push my butt back fully in the seat in rough seas.

There is a bow-mounted casting tower located on the forward hatch, which is fastened with a turnbuckle. I had fallen off a standard platform the previous season and severed a tendon in my foot. In rough seas you have to be one of the Wallendas to stay up on those things. After pushing one of my grandsons on a swing at the park, I installed a swing seat on the frame that I sit on to remain comfortable when posted up and waiting for fish to show. Unlike most seats, it swings back and out of the way when I stand up to cast. Over the years I've learned that a dash of comfort on the skiff makes me perform better during a long day on the water.

Because I often fish alone, I rely on my bow-mounted 82-pound thrust 24-volt Motor Guide trolling motor a lot to get into position. With an extension handle and foot-operated cutoff switch mounted to the floor of the bow tower, I am able

View of the bow-mounted casting tower, attached to the forward hatch with a turnbuckle. SHANNON BROUILETTE PHOTO

to maneuver the skiff and fish without missing a beat—at least that's the case when everything works correctly. Trolling motors were the bane of my existence until Motor Guide came out with their digital ones. Though I keep two spares at the house, I have yet to have a problem with one.

Boat Gear

In addition to the gear I bring on the boat each day for fishing—rods, reels, and flies—I like to start each day with a full tank of fuel (you never know how far you might have to run), oil, fully–charged trolling-motor batteries, and ice in the chest. Here are some other things that I consider essential to have on the boat.

GPS. A GPS can be helpful during the early season when predawn trips typically average 15 to 20 miles. In addition to tracking the course, the GPS lets me find the warmer, 72- to 74-degree water that tarpon seek. Once the season is in full stride, I use the GPS a lot less because finding warm enough water is not a factor and the runs are short. However, the need to rely on GPS varies from one fishery to another. For example, in Homosassa even seasoned captains use a GPS to navigate through rock piles on the way to the fishing grounds during low tide.

Safety and emergency gear. In addition to the normal Coast Guard–required flotation devices, I always have an **inflatable SOS fanny pack,** which was a thoughtful gift from my son and one you might put on your gift list for boaters you care about. I wear this when I am fishing alone, especially when crossing open water like Boca Grande Pass before daybreak. The small CO_2 cartridge only inflates the flotation device when it hits the water, and you can wear it easily around your shoulders or waist (depending on the model) without it getting in your way. I also have a small tool kit with a Phillips-head screwdriver, Vise Grips, pliers, and some duct tape, as well as spotlights, flares, and first-aid kit.

Kill switches are safety devices with straps attached to them that you wear around your wrist. When the switch is pulled out, the engine stops. Because these straps are prone to tangling around the steering wheel or control handles, most people do not wear them. I think they are a necessity when boating alone or if my grandkids are on

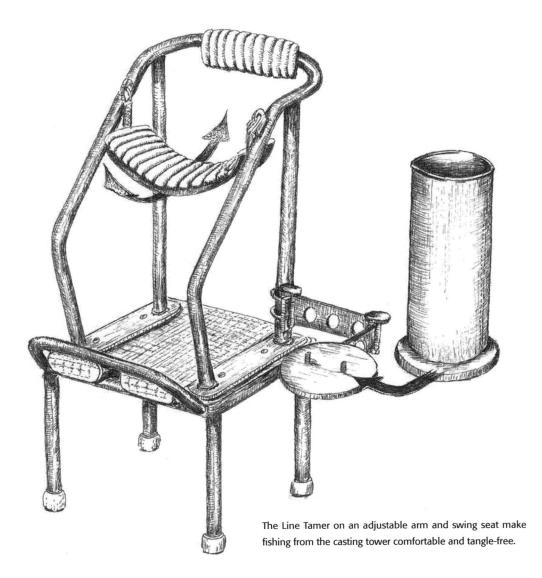

The Line Tamer on an adjustable arm and swing seat make fishing from the casting tower comfortable and tangle-free.

The author's quick-release anchor system.

board; so to keep the strap out of the way I clip the cord to a wide Velcro band marketed for jet skis, and wear it on my ankle. This makes it comfortable and easy to put on or remove.

Water. You can't have too much water on board. I also carry Gatorade to replace lost electrolytes in the extreme heat. Newcomers, especially, tend to not drink enough during the day. Severe dehydration can ruin your entire trip. Make sure you drink lots of water (and eat snacks) when the fishing is slow so that you are at your best when it is not.

Fly Line Tamer. I love things that work, and this product by Pro Trim does exactly what it claims to do. First, it keeps the line properly stacked inside the cylinder, out of harm's way and out of the wind. When moving from one location to another in relatively calm seas, you can leave the fly rod in the cylinder so it is ready to use when you get to your next spot. The nonskid bottom keeps the device from sliding around the floor. In addition, I can relocate to the stern of the skiff and cast without worrying about my fly line tangling or hanging up on countless things in the back of the boat. First-time users sometimes have trouble stripping line back into the cylinder. If you strip the first length of line into the Line Tamer, the rest will follow. Because I spend most of my time propped up in the bow tower, I mounted the Line Tamer at the proper height on a swivel bracket. I stow the Line Tamer on the deck when running.

Anchor system. Once you hook a tarpon, you generally take chase. After the tarpon's initial jumps, it is going to take fly line and backing at an alarming rate. Every second counts. Retrieving the anchor or scrambling around while undoing the line only gives the tarpon a greater head start and reduces your odds for success. I attach my anchor line to an eyelet on the bow deck of my skiff with a Wichard snap shackle available from West Marine (look in the sailing section of their catalog). I replaced the pull cord with a longer length of weed-eater line and a small wood ball on the end. Because the anchor rope is most often under tension, a yank of the weed-eater line opens the shackle and the line springs free and away from the skiff. Just below the shackle, a short length of smaller rope holds a Styrofoam crab-trap marker that floats so I can retrieve the anchor upon my return.

A 6-foot section of bungee rope in between the shackle and the anchor rope takes the initial shock out of the anchor system coming taut in heavy seas, which makes for a much more stable fishing platform in rough conditions. From the end of the bungee line, I attach an anchor rope to the chain and anchor using a loop-to-loop connection. I can loop in a section of additional line if I need more length in deeper or faster moving water. This system has proven to be invaluable, and I have yet to have the shackle to fail to pop open easily when needed or to open inadvertently under pressure.

Kill gaff. I carry one, but you do not need to if you are not concerned about a record fish. A kill gaff and a lip gaff are two different animals, and you can't substitute one for the other. A kill gaff is only good for killing fish. Anglers use lip gaffs to lift fish, but I prefer to grab their jaws because I think that putting a hole in the tarpon's mouth inhibits their ability to feed. Some anglers argue that to grab a fish you must fight a fish longer and if you use a lip gaff you can boat them when they are still green, but I do not agree with that.

Push pole. I often pole the boat when another angler is on board, but I use the trolling motor when fishing alone.

Extras. Two pair of sunglasses, sunscreen, Advil, and extra hat. I carry a hook file and small pair of scissors for trimming flies in my pocket, and fishing pliers on my belt.

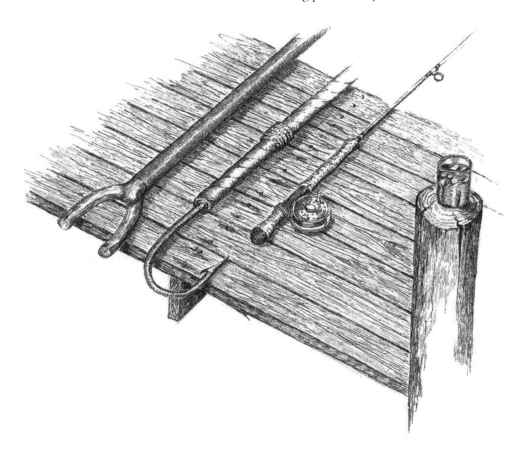

A Good Day to Stay Home

There were more clouds than sky and the wind was a solid 20 knots out of the south/southeast, but for reasons I regret I had to take a look in a spot that required an open-water crossing in my wood skiff. I pulled away from the dock with Merle Haggard's words and melody playing over and over in my mind: *I think I'll just stay here and drink . . .*

As I entered the sound and the first wave rolled over the port-side gunnel, I thought, *This skiff was not built for this.* I turned the nose more into the wind and pressed ahead. The rub rails looked like they were on springs. I stepped to the starboard side of the flat bottom to force the chine down in the slop. I was soaking wet now. The late December water was cold. The wind made it colder. It seemed like forever before I finally turned behind the lee of the outside island. I stood on the rear deck with the kill switch strapped to my wrist and idled the rest of the way.

When I arrived at the flat, foam from the cresting waves weaved across the surface of the coffee-colored water.

The drill was simple. I balanced on the forward casting platform with my fly rod in hand. My body was a spinnaker in the howling wind. As long as I stayed up there, the bow continued to aim down sea. If I stepped down, the boat began to come around. I lowered the foot of the outboard and set it straight, hoping it would act as a rudder. Each swell lifted the stern and lowered the bow as it rolled under. Eventually, I adjusted to the rhythm of the rocking boat.

On the third drift, I saw the first tarpon bust, which raised my spirits for a fourth. *If there's one tarpon here I can catch it,* I reasoned—a thought that seems foolish now, of course, but one that made perfect sense at the time, given the circumstances and my need for optimism. I heard a tarpon free jump behind the skiff and turned back in time to see the hole in the water she cut

20 yards straight off the transom. I saw the second jump and gauged her girth as she entered the backside of a wave, estimating her well over a hundred pounds. I don't have the slightest clue why tarpon free jump, nor do I know why they often do it repeatedly directly on the same course, but this fish was giving me a good show. I recall thinking, *A third jump and she might get a little too close for comfort.*

Ten feet back, she came up and directly at me. I was still poised on the casting deck in the stern when she did what I deemed impossible—she turned sideways in midair. I am convinced she saw me in flight. I yelled as the two rear struts of the poling platform took the full force of the collision. The skiff vanished under me, and I crashed to the floor aft of the center seat, convinced the tarpon had boarded my boat. But, thank goodness, she did not. She would have taken apart what took four months to build.

I was still sprawled on the floor when I felt the stern coming around hard in the wind. Water began pouring over the portside gunnel at an alarming rate. *How could things have gone so wrong so fast, I wondered?* I scrambled to my feet, gathered myself and with what few wits I had left, started the outboard, pulled the drain plugs, and went home. Merle Haggard had a good idea after all.

Running the Boat

ishermen are like porcupines huddled together on a cold night. No matter how hard they try to get close, they can't help sticking one another. Conflicts often occur when a newcomer to the fishery is thrown into the mix, and most of the problems revolve around how you run the boat.

A cadet doesn't stand much of a chance in a new fishing ground. It's like the fellow strolling through the city zoo who is shocked to see a lamb and a lion locked in the same cage. After fetching the zookeeper, the man points to the cage and asks, "How the heck does that work?"

"It works fine," the zookeeper responds, "as long as we toss in a new lamb every two days."

When we sold our vacation home on Florida's east coast and purchased a place in Boca Grande, I was the lamb. Though new on this water, I fortunately had two close friends who were established anglers in the area: Charlie Madden, a recreational fisherman, and Tommy Locke, a professional guide. Both of them helped me break some of the ice with the locals, but there was still a lot that needed to be chipped away before I could join the fishing community.

Joining the community may or may not be important to you, but for me it is essential. Over time, anyone can learn how to fish an area without help from others, but who would want to? Making friends and building relationships is far and away the number one by-product of fishing.

In time, local guides Leo Henriques, Zeke Sieglaff, and Tommy Locke took me into their confidence by sharing information. I tried desperately to return the favors, but in those early years I didn't have much to offer. They didn't keep score. It wasn't about math with them. It was about trust, respect, friendship, and courtesy.

Locals and working guides have a responsibility to do the right thing on the water. This does not absolve the first-timer who runs too close to your boat, but running too close would be a much bigger offense if a local guide did the same thing. The more knowledgeable you are about your fishery, the less acceptable it is to make mistakes that cost others fish.

Rules of the Road

Last year I spoke with a fellow angler who was going through this break-in period. He was frustrated and tired of being yelled at. Here are a few basic rules of the road we discussed, and they all revolve around being aware of your surroundings and being courteous. You have to want to do the right thing on the water.

Study the Lineup

Before barging into an active fishing area, study the fleet from afar with a pair of binoculars. To determine the line and direction of incoming tarpon, watch the guide on the poling platform to see which way he is looking. Look at which way the angler's rod is pointing. Then, look at the boat behind them, and you can quickly get an idea of the direction that they are expecting the fish to come from. Once you've determined the direction of the action, come in quietly and *behind* all the other boats in the line. Do not come in front of these anglers and cut off the fish.

Determine the Line of Travel

In trout fishing, in fresh and salt water, you have specific spots that are good and some that are bad. As long as someone doesn't come along and cast in the spot that you are fishing, you can share the water. But tarpon fishing is a lot different. Unlike the normal trout stream, tarpon anglers are often fishing for fish that are coming rather than fish that are already there. Because the fish are often moving, you can get in someone's "spot" without even knowing it even when you move in to an area 200 or 300 yards away. Depending on the line the fish are taking, your arrival to an area can cut or alter the course of the fish. Again, be conscious of how others are set up and mindful of the direction they are fishing and don't get in front or alter the course of "their" fish.

It helps to have some basic understanding of the traveling patterns of the tarpon in the fishery.

For instance, in Boca Grande, Boca Grande Pass is like the hub of the beach fishery. If you are on the beach and north of Boca Grande Pass, most of the fish are traveling south to the pass. If you are south of the pass, it is plausible to think that most of the fish are traveling north. This is not always the case, such as when fish exit the pass to go offshore to spawn, but that is not the norm. Knowledge of the general patterns combined with observing how the anglers are posted up will help you figure out where the front of the line is and keep you in good standing with fellow anglers.

Determining the line the fish are taking before making a move can give you a second option for setting up. Don't always assume the bulk of the approaching fish are in the center of the fleet. Though they may have been there earlier, fishing pressure can (and most likely will) alter the course of the fish. Take time to study the water around you. You might have landed in a silver mine by being on the outside of the fray. Try working the far outside edges of the concentration of skiffs, making sure not to cut off the flow of tarpon to others.

Swing Wide

Yes, the shortest distance between two points is a straight line, but do not run through or near other anglers working fish. Every fishing area is different, so it's hard to say what the best distance is, but that distance should always be measured in lengths of football fields. It may take you a little out of the way, but it will take you a long way down the road to earning respect of fellow anglers. Many of these offenses come from pleasure boaters, and it is important to keep things in perspective when someone spoils your fishing. Everyone has a right to use the water, and many times pleasure boaters have no idea that you are posted up on a run.

Kill the Engine

Use your trolling motor or push pole to enter and exit active fishing grounds. In most cases, you

Working with others.

should kill the engine when you are 100 yards or more from the closest boat. In Homosassa, if you can discern a skiff's color, you should not be running the outboard. Also use your trolling motor to leave. Just because you're done doesn't mean everyone else is.

When you hook up, there is normally time to exit an area without cranking up immediately (perhaps with the exception of giant fish heading for places unknown). Chasing after a tarpon in a panic is generally not a veteran move. The fish's path can easily be determined with a quick study, and her speed judged with a glance at the angler's reel.

Hooked Up

The angler cannot control a fish's direction in the first part of the fight, and as a boater in the area, you should do everything within reason to make way for anglers pursuing a hooked fish. When a boat releases its anchor and leaves the buoy in pursuit of a hooked tarpon, you should not set up in its spot.

Being Guided

Guides lump clients in different categories; for example, those who can and cannot cast. Then there are clients from out of town and locals. You can bet the dude from Ohio is more likely to see prime fishing areas by a guide than the client who just bought a condo in the area.

It is bad form to return to areas learned when fishing with a guide without his approval. If you hire a guide planning on picking up some hotspots, you should be honest with the guide from the start. Most guides appreciate this and will assist newcomers in finding fish as well as the rules of courtesy, which can vary from one fishery to the next.

Humor Helps

Now and again I do well to remind myself that I'm actually doing this for fun, and it's not worth having another heart attack simply because someone fails to be considerate. Don't get me wrong. I still have no problem giving someone a piece of my mind. The problem is I've been doing this a

When you see a boat posted up, and the two anglers are looking in one direction, enter behind them so you do not cut off their fish. MARK HATTER PHOTO

long time, and I'm starting to wonder how many more pieces of my mind I should give away—I didn't start out with enough to be giving them away carelessly.

Boat Running Tips

Boat handling is critical not only for feeding and fighting fish, but also catching fish. Everyone congratulates the guy who caught the big fish, but that is only half of the deal. The guy who handled the boat is the other half—perhaps even more than that. Teamwork is so important that the odds of landing a 200-pound fish without a good captain are pretty small. While running a boat is fun, I see a lot of anglers do things that cost them tarpon because of the way they operate their boats. For more tips on handling a boat when fighting fish, see page 126 in the chapter "Fighting Fish."

Boat Slap

When waves hit the boat, they also bounce back. Every wave that bounces off the transom or hull telegraphs your location to the tarpon and can spook them. If you notice that all the fish are rolling 200 feet away from you, then boat slap might be the culprit.

To minimize boat slap in choppy water, anchor or stake down so the bow faces into the sea whenever possible. Sometimes anchoring stern first offers casting advantages or improved visibility. I prefer looking directly forward from my bow platform whenever practical. Looking over the length of the boat toward the stern means I've got to spot the fish a boat length farther out before they shy away, which can be difficult in low light.

When I post up stern first, I tie the anchor line off one corner of the transom. The 90-degree corner facing into the waves reduces slap more than the flat transom. I also lift the foot of the outboard as high as possible. Waves glancing off the lower unit can sound like an echo chamber.

Not all skiffs are created equal when it comes to hull slap. My flat-bottomed wood skiff slaps like a Baptist date at the drive-inn movie when I stand in the stern with the waves coming toward the bow. I can reduce the noise by moving to the stern, and when I lean the skiff over on the chine it's as quiet as a mouse.

Anchor Strategies

Sometimes when the wind and current move in opposite directions, the anchor line doesn't come taut and the boat can't settle into position, which makes presentations to approaching fish more difficult and challenging. If you anchor the skiff so the transom faces the current, the blunt surface offers greater resistance to the flow and can help you stabilize the boat. Be careful though—strong tidal currents can draw the stern under. Also, never attempt to anchor in strong tidal flow with an anchor forward and aft. A skiff positioned sideways to the flow can turn over easily.

When anchored, you sometimes need to make minor adjustments to the skiff's angle, which you can do easily by turning the foot of your engine. The lower unit acts like a rudder in fast moving tidal flow.

It Takes One to Know One

The boat handler needs to know the fly caster's needs in order for them to make a good team, and he should have a complete understanding of fly fishing. This might sound obvious, but a lot of guides do not specialize in fly fishing. The caster and the boat handler are a team, and each player has specific duties. Because he is calling the shots on the platform, the boat handler must determine how good a "shot" the caster is. If the person on the bow can't cast very far, is inaccurate, or takes too much time to get the fly in front of the fish, the handler has to adapt and deal with those shortcomings. It's tough to make any real improvements in casting during the heat of battle.

When an angler hooks up and eventually takes chase, you should not move in to his spot.

For instance, let's suppose that you generously offer to help a friend of a friend catch his first tarpon. Since he is the guest, you have been working hard, poling him around the flats. Earlier in the day, you had a few shots at fish and could see that the caster was fairly accurate out to about 55 to 60 feet, but he took too many false-casts to get the fly in the water. The friend of the friend is working really hard, and you are having a fine time, but it is clear that you are not going to get him to cast farther or with fewer false-casts, at least on that day.

In the afternoon, a 15-mile-per-hour wind picks up, blowing from port to starboard. You spot a string of fish approaching at about 10:00, and you determine that they should pass across the bow no more than 25 feet out. But the best angle of presentation is at about 50 feet, well before the fish get that close. You alert the caster and begin spinning the skiff to the left, yelling, "Fish at 10:00, cast!!!" The caster makes one false-cast, then two, and then three, finally delivering a cast that piles up about 35 feet from the boat. He is disappointed that he blew the shot. And, your disappointment also shows.

What happened? Though the quartering presentation you wanted would have been a much higher percentage play, you, the boat handler, sabotaged the situation. You knew the caster took too many false-casts, and yet you took the option that required a quick delivery. Second, that 55-foot cast he could make in still conditions that morning was just reduced to 35 feet into the quartering 15-mile-per-hour wind. Though the friend of a friend blew the shot, you blew the call. Due to the caster's skill level, the 90-degree shot at 25 feet

with a left-to-right crossing wind was actually a better bet.

Keep the Boat Clean and Clear

Line management is critical in tarpon fishing. Snags and tangles are devastating when casting and clearing line. It's important that you deliver the cast accurately and quickly, and nothing brings a sinking feeling to your belly faster than watching your fly stop about halfway between you and where you wanted it to go as a wad of running line slams against your stripping guide or catches a boat cleat. Well, nothing except for getting that

It's important that you deliver the cast accurately and quickly, and nothing brings a sinking feeling to your belly faster than watching your fly stop about halfway between you and where you wanted it to go as a wad of running line slams against your stripping guide or catches a boat cleat. MARK HATTER PHOTO

perfect presentation and eat, setting the hook, and as the 140-pound fish tears away, having your line catch on the Velcro straps of your sandals, despite your best efforts to dance on the bow to try and prevent exactly that thing from happening.

You need to anticipate that the towel, fly rack, boat bag, or rod that wasn't stowed away will catch your fly line. Stand up in the back of the boat, identify things that are going to get in the way, and put them where they won't.

Respect Others' Boats

One of the nice things about working with a guide is that you can let him worry about the boatwork while you focus on the fishing. But the day will go a lot better if you dip your *nonmarking* soles in the water before stepping aboard and wipe them off with the towel that the guide will most likely provide. If he doesn't offer one, ask.

Most professional guides think of their skiffs as their offices, and you would too if your livelihood depends on fire, oxygen, and fuel all meeting at the same instant at 4:00 AM. For those of us who don't make a living fishing, it is only a major pain in the rear if the engine doesn't start or something goes wrong. For a guide, the boat not starting or running right can add up to two hundred mosquito bites, three busted knuckles, and a full day's lost wages. That's the reason your guide might not be talking much on the long ride home at the end of the day. He's listening to the drone of his engine to make sure it sounds the same that night as the other 250-plus trips before. Let him listen. It's the only shot he's got of getting a decent night's sleep.

Watch the Wake

Flip Pallot taught me years ago not to ride in the wake of another boat if it can be avoided. All of the unused fuel and oil from the boat in front of you winds up in a haze on your sunglasses. When you arrive at your next fishing spot, you'll spend

five minutes trying to get them clean instead of looking for tarpon. If you must trail another skiff, steer over to the upwind side of the wake so the unwanted residue is blown clear by the time it gets to you.

Making Tight Turns

A skiff at idle speed will turn in a much tighter axis when the lower unit is tilted upward. The higher you lift the lower unit, the tighter the skiff will turn. Experiment by turning the wheel full to the port or starboard while idling, and begin lifting the lower unit. Note the smaller circumference of your circle as you trim up the engine. A portion of the propulsion from your prop pushes the transom down while also lifting the bow, which causes the stern to become more of a pivot point when turning.

Keeping your angler in a position where he can pull directly behind a hooked tarpon takes some maneuvering. Tilting the lower unit can help. However, trimming the engine too high disables your ability to stop your forward motion by using reverse. In reverse, a raised lower unit lowers the stern and raises the bow instead of stopping your forward motion. Adding power will only cause cavitation—the prop doesn't get a grip on the water—and you lose control.

Throwing in the Towel

Most skiffs with cockpits have a sump area aft where any water is delivered to the bilge and pumped out of the boat. If you keep a towel handy for cleaning up during the day, don't leave it on the floor. One day I took a huge wave over the bow, which filled the cockpit half full of seawater. You've got it. The towel was washed to the sump exit and plugged up the only hope I had of sending the water to the bilge. Fortunately, I realized the problem and removed the towel before taking on another wave.

Making Do

Charlie Madden and I were each posted on the same run on the Gulf well south of Boca Grande Pass. Though there was a good push of fish, and we were both hooking tarpon with regularity, the afternoon sea breeze had kicked up, causing every third wave or so to wash over the decks, and there wasn't much light remaining. Thinking about the 10-mile run home, I pulled anchor and twirled my finger above my head to indicate that I was cranking up. Charlie did the same.

We were running side by side at a good clip when Charlie's skiff lost control and whipped around in a frightening circle. Charlie cut power, and I idled back to investigate. The sea was pushing both skiffs dangerously close to the beach. It was almost dark. He dropped anchor, and I tied off to his starboard side, our rub rails banging together.

The problem was obvious. The plate attaching the engine to the steering cable rod had rusted clean through. I'm not great about taking care of my stuff, but my pal Charlie Madden stinks when it comes to taking care of his equipment. "Oh crap," exclaimed Charlie, "We've really got a problem here!"

I looked back at my steering plate, which was intact and free of rust. "No Charlie, *we* don't have a problem here, but *you* are sure in a heck of a mess."

We both managed a laugh, even though the situation was not a laughing matter, and then we discussed our options. Charlie wasn't going to leave his skiff. I agreed. I would not have left mine. Any attempt to pull Charlie's skiff back across Boca Grande Pass was out of the question. There was a hard outgoing tide pushing against the howling west wind. Pulling his boat in that sea at night across the pass would be foolhardy.

"I've got an idea," I said to Charlie, rummaging through the contents of my forward hatch for a boat mop with a wood handle. I held it up proudly.

"Thank God," Charlie replied. "You found a mop. What a relief!"

Ignoring his sarcastic remark, I tied a mooring line to one end of the handle and began lashing it to the port side of the engine cowling near the base. When I tied off the last bit of line, it was surprisingly secure.

"Son of a gun, I think that will work," Charlie said, grinning from ear to ear.

We crossed the pass without incident. Charlie worked the controls with his right hand and the mop handle with his left, running on his usual speed—high.

Back at his dock, we laughed over a well-deserved drink. Charlie knew a mechanic who might be able to make the repairs that night. "See you on the water in the morning," I called out and drove the remaining 5 miles to my dock.

The next morning I left the house well before daybreak. The spot I wanted to fish was 20 miles south, and I wanted to be the first one there. When I pulled off the throttle and began idling in, I could just make out the form of a skiff. "This isn't good," I muttered to no one in particular. As I came in with the trolling motor, I recognized Charlie's skiff.

"See you got the boat repaired," I yelled.

Charlie stepped back to the stern and lifted the mop handle: "Naw, the guy wasn't home. I might just leave it this way . . . sort of got used to it now!"

CHAPTER SEVEN

The Hunt

Whether posted up on the beach waiting to ambush fish cruising by or silently poling or motoring along with electrics in the backcountry looking for laid-up fish, tarpon fishing is a lot like hunting. I like to think of posting up like hunting out of a tree stand. You pick a good spot and just wait for your quarry to come within range. Slip hunting—stalking slowly through the woods— is a lot like trying to find laid-up or rolling fish in the backcountry.

And like in hunting, "spots" are sacred. Generally, you are better off asking someone about their sex life or how much money they made last year than where they are tarpon fishing in the morning. When I try to explain the importance of fishing spots to someone new to the game, I like to tell the following joke.

Two buddies were fishing from the bank, staring at their lifeless bobbers, when one inquired, "You and me are friends, right"?

"You betcha!" the other nodded.

"Okay. If you had two trucks wouldcha give me one of 'em?"

"Heck yeah," the friend replied. "If I had two pickups, I'd give you one. Yer my best friend."

Following a short pause, the other asked, "If you had two boats, wouldcha give me one of them too?"

"Sure. I ain't even got one boat, but if I had two, I'd give you one," he gladly responded.

Finally, following a thoughtful and considerably longer pause, the other asked, "So, what if you had two hawgs? I reckon you'd give me one of them, right?"

"That ain't fair," his buddy scowled. "You know darn well I got two hawgs!"

• • •

To be able to find your own spots and learn about the fishery on your own is one of the most rewarding aspects of fishing. Discovery is everything, because things don't stay the same for too long. It's a cliché to say that a particular guide "knows the water like the back of his hand." But when I hear that, I always think that unlike the back of our

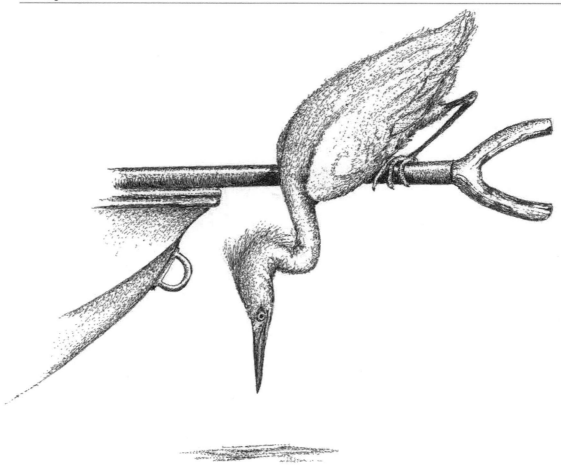

hands, water and the bottom changes. You need to learn and relearn some of it every year.

I understand why there are hotspot maps for sale and magazine editors want articles with maps that show people where to go. Lots of people do not have the time to figure out great spots on their own because their time is limited. The problem is, "The Spot" does not exist. You cannot even go to the most reliable fishing areas day after day and catch tarpon at any given time of the day and any given time of the tide.

A vast body of water such as the Florida Keys, Boca Grande, or even Mosquito Lagoon can appear overwhelming at first glance. My son, Billy, hit the nail on the head when he described his mental approach to breaking down one large fishery into a series of small lakes, which is just a figure of speech for all the little basins that may be divided by sandbars, channels, mangrove islands, and so on. Commit your time and efforts to learning one lake at a time. Eventually you will understand the tarpon's travel patterns between the lakes.

Slip Hunting the Backcountry

Fishing for laid-up tarpon is slip hunting at its best. You are moving quietly through the water as you look for fish that are holding in the water. It can take a long time to cover water as you creep along. Most of the casts are short, no more than 25 to 30 feet. Not only is accuracy critical, you must lay the fly in that magic zone—2 feet in front of the fish's face. In the calm water, your presentations also must be delicate, and I often use a lighter rod such as a 10-weight.

The most effective way to fish for laid-up fish is by teaming up, with one person poling and the other person fishing. The person poling can see better high up on the poling platform, and he can easily maneuver the boat into the best position for the angler casting and feeding the fish. If you are fishing alone, your only option is to use a trolling motor, which can be a real challenge because you can't easily stop or reposition the boat for the best presentation.

Most good backcountry spots have water depths from 5 to 8 feet and share some common characteristics. Most spots have long corridors of sand bottoms lined with eel-grass flats that provide good highways for fish to move along and nearby islands or protruding sand or oyster bars provide protection from wind. These are big fish, and adult tarpon aren't prone to swim up narrow, shallow creeks that might become impassable on lower tides, so areas that have good tidal flows and easy access are key.

Oddly enough, tarpon and green turtles often share the same backcountry waters. When I first became aware of this I was fishing in Mosquito Lagoon, but I have seen it many times in Boca Grande and Homosassa. Tarpon seem to settle in near the area where green turtles pop up for air. Of course it may be the other way around. It took me a while to figure out that the turtles were disturbing the grass beds with their flippers, scaring shrimp, crabs, and baitfish for the tarpon's dining pleasure. I am always pleased to see turtles in the areas I am working.

Visibility

Even if the spot holds fish, you need to select the ones that work best for you. I know of places that often hold large concentrations of fish, but the dark bottoms make them unfishable, unless the fish are showing on top. Fish swimming over dark grass beds are hard to see, so it makes more sense to set up in an area with white sand bottoms that make the fish easier to spot. Fish are also easier to see and catch in shallower areas. Often I will leave the main concentration of fish to find fewer but more catchable tarpon skirting the shallower bars or edges.

In the backcountry, many different fly patterns can work well. Most of the stuff tarpon eat either live or grow up in the grass-bed flats. This includes baitfish, but shrimp, crabs, sea horses, and mantis shrimp reside there as well. In addition to baitfish imitations, critter-type flies are often a good choice for backcountry fish.

Laid-Up Tarpon

Tarpon can lay up on the beach or in the backcountry, but it is most common to hunt laid-up fish in the backcountry. Though tarpon can lay up at different depths, the easiest way to spot them is during calm conditions when they are finned out. They suspend at about 30 degrees with their tails higher than their heads, their tails and dorsal fins protruding above the surface as they face into the tidal flow.

The higher the sun, the better the visibility. I always check the direction of the sun before moving into a backwater bay, and I enter from the direction that offers the best visibility. White, puffy clouds reflect off the water's surface and make visibility nearly impossible. Look for blue sky, and fish the water in that direction. A black cloud on the horizon with good sun to your back will light up a flat like a stage.

Laid-up tarpon hold facing the current, so it is important to figure out the speed and direction of the tidal flow before fishing an area.

Laid-up tarpon hold facing the current, so it is important to figure out the speed and direction of the tidal flow before fishing an area. Study a crab-trap marker or piling. Is the marker straining against its line? Is the current eddying around the piling? Which way is it flowing, and to what extent? Stop the boat and look at floating grass or leaves on the water. Drop your fly in the water with the leader and butt section perpendicular to the water movement. Is there a bend forming in the line? How fast is it pulling the fly downcurrent? Once you have answered these questions, you know what direction the tarpon are facing and how far to lead them. Laid-up fish don't move, but the tide does.

When searching for laid-up fish, do not look too far ahead of the skiff. In calm conditions, glance around occasionally for the tip of a dorsal fin or tail above the surface, but direct your attention under the surface just ahead and to either side of the skiff. Move slowly and quietly. If you are working a trolling motor and the visibility allows, work the skiff into the wind. This will help stop the forward progress of the boat if you should spot a fish directly ahead. In most cases, the fish you see under the surface will be within a few boat lengths away. Three boat lengths would be a gift.

As usual the person on the poling platform has an advantage due to height; however, there is a different twist with laid-up fish. The fish you're hunting will be close. The view just ahead of the skiff may not be as good for the guide as it is for the angler. It's like sitting in a skybox and not being able to see over the rail. The angler should be poised on the casting platform, paying close attention to this blind spot.

Focus on anything under the surface that does not fit in with the environment. You may only see the top half of a tail. Remember, the 30 degrees? The tail is the highest anatomy of the tarpon in the water column. It often has a hint of red coloring on the edges. In any event, you will see a tarpon part before you see the entire fish. It will materialize before you. Before you see it, you can't imagine a 120-pound fish could be there. After you see it, you can't imagine it being anywhere else.

This is when most anglers want to speed things up. They shift into panic mode to get the fly in front of the fish. It rarely works out well. A good guide will stop the skiff and slow the angler down. As long as the tarpon is unaware of your presence, it probably isn't going anywhere. At this point,

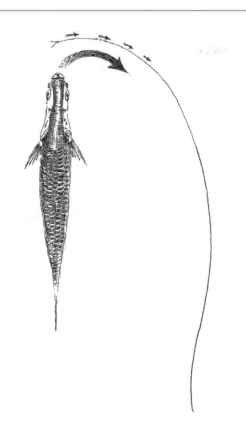

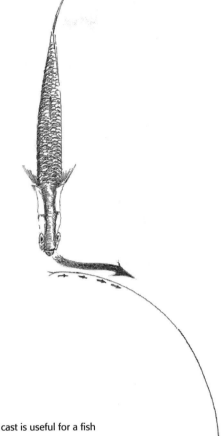

things should almost be done in slow motion. The guide should maneuver the skiff according to the position of the fish and the abilities of the angler.

Remember checking the tidal flow before you started your search? After considering how the flow and direction will influence your presentation, pick a spot on the water about three feet in front of the tarpon. Do not look at the fish when you cast, or your fly will hit its head every time. Draw a mental picture of a 2-foot cube teetering out and on top of the tarpon's nose. The trick is to deliver the fly in a natural, lifelike manner to the inside of the imaginary cube. Watch the fish's reaction. If it turns and follows, the game is on.

One of the best casts for laid-up tarpon is the curve cast, especially when tarpon are either facing away or directly toward you. When the fish is fac-

A curve cast is useful for a fish that is facing directly away from or directly facing you.

ing away from you, a curve cast prevents you from lining the fish. When the fish is facing you, a curve cast leads the fish 90 degrees to one side rather than straight at the boat, which could spook it. Many times moving the skiff into a better position for a regular cast is not an option due to glare or bow slap. The curve cast is so effective in these situations because it is a low-profile, sidearm cast.

Casts to laid-up fish must be delicate. Because their eyes are more on top of their heads than on the sides, tarpon look up and forward. A tarpon laid up on the surface, facing you from a boat length away, can easily see you high on the bow of the skiff waving a 9-foot stick in the air with 15 feet of line on the end. This is tender fishing where crouching, minimum motion, few back-casts, and low gentle rod movements are all critical for success.

Midmorning's higher sun brings about sight-fishing opportunities. One of the most difficult de-cisions of the day is at hand. Do you leave fish to find fish? Your choice can be made easier by paying close attention to what the tarpon are saying. Are the tarpon around you as happy as they were at daybreak? Odds are they're not. Once a fish or two has been launched or other anglers join in the fray,

the fish often drop down lower in the water col-umn. How long has it been since a quality presen-tation paid off with a hook-up? Staying in an area with uneasy fish rarely pays off. As time ticks away, better light conditions heighten the lure of sight-fishing opportunities on the beach with clear water and sandy white bottoms. A whole new set of challenging decisions are on the horizon as you make the trip out of the backcountry.

Posting Up on the Beach

Posting up is an exciting and complex game and can best be compared to hunting from a tree stand and waiting for game to come within range. As with hunting out of a tree stand, location is critical for success. In general, fish on the beach are going somewhere and moving most of the time.

Even if they aren't migrating, tarpon travel almost constantly and settle into an area only briefly to feed or rest before moving on to another. Tarpon navigate by following the contours of the bottom formed by sandbars or rip currents much the way deer follow game trails. The clear water on the beach makes it easier to see the traffic patterns of fish, but they also follow bottom contours in the backcountry.

Bottom contours are to tarpon as roads are to us. Think of the roads you drive day in and day out on your way to and from work or to the hardware store. When those roads change or someone puts up a detour sign, you are forced to change course to reach your destination. The same

is true for traveling tarpon, only their roads change more often. Tarpon migration routes are like major freeways, and everyday local movement should be viewed as fish taking the back roads.

Tides trigger fish to move, and anglers must learn how to constantly adjust their positions as the water rises or falls. Sandbars and cuts that tarpon frequent during high water may be impassable during lower tides. On the other hand, low tide may force tarpon to take the longer road around to get from point A to point B. It's the same when driving a skiff during low tides to get to a specific spot. As a result, traveling fish are often concentrated in tighter corridors during falling or low tides. When fishing runs on rising tides, watch areas

Tarpon migration routes are like major freeways, and everyday local movement should be viewed as fish taking the back roads.

where fish can cross over bars that were too shallow an hour before. The flow of tides and volume of water transfer varies during the moon phases. As a rule tarpon push best on the strongest tides.

Just about the time you begin to figure out a few spots, a hurricane or tropical storm blows through and changes the area so much that you must learn it all over again. That's the bad news. The good news is that same storm may have pushed the sand around sufficiently in another area to make a new fishing spot. Sometimes, after a big storm, it's worth going back and checking those marginal spots—they might be great. Because of Mother Nature, you never completely get it all figured out.

But Mother Nature doesn't have everything to do with it. I'll never forget one year in Boca Grande where they pumped in a lot of sand to improve the beaches. As all that sand began to erode off the beach, it created these ledges that extended out into the Gulf of Mexico. For perhaps a month, fishing these ledges was pay dirt. No nautical chart would have shown them.

In the late winter, while water temperatures are still too cool for tarpon to show, I often take a boat ride to inspect prime water and to try and find some new spots. Going out during the middle of a sunny day gives you a chance to study the bottom contours. Winter tides are generally lower and the water is clearer because the cold has killed the algae blooms that are everpresent in the summer.

When fishing runs, pay special attention to points or sharp turns along the edges of bars. Tarpon follow these edges, but they don't hug the exact perimeter of the drop offs. When a drop-off edge turns abruptly, it's not uncommon for the lead fish to continue ahead for a short distance before angling back to the edge of the bar. These are prime ambush points from which to get a good angle on a fish rather than a head-on shot.

All sorts of things can influence the pattern of the fish, from structure such as rock piles or sand bars to another fisherman's boat in the line, pleasure boaters a quarter mile away, or sharks. Keep your eyes open and don't be afraid to pull away from a reliable fishing spot and go after fish that

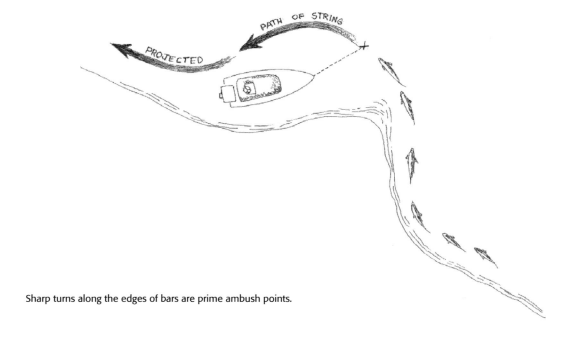

Sharp turns along the edges of bars are prime ambush points.

are clearly showing in the distance. They are there for a reason. and if you can figure out what that reason is, you'll have learned something valuable.

Seeing Fish

Some people see fish better than others, but everyone sees better under the water with a quality pair of polarized glasses. I like amber or copper tints. Sunny days make it a lot easier to see the fish from farther away, giving you plenty of time to get prepared for the best shot. On cloudy days, you can still catch fish, but they seem to sneak up on you and you must be ready to cast quickly.

Even on bright days, tarpon are tougher to see when they are swimming sideways to you. Like bonefish swimming over white sand, they blend in with their surroundings. Anglers often think they are seeing fish suspended over sandy bottoms, when in reality they are seeing their shadows. Because their backs are dark, they are much easier to see while swimming toward or directly away from you.

Glassy, hazy days and low light can make it incredibly hard to see. Flat water is like a mirror reflecting the sun, clouds, and haze. A slight ripple reduces that reflection and makes it easier to see. In the late afternoon when the sun is low in the horizon, try looking into and through the face of waves that are angling toward the sun, instead of over the top of them. In this instance, they are facing the sun, and it is similar to looking at a flat surface with high overhead sun. You can also try lifting the hinged arms of the glasses off your ears and letting them rest against the sides of your hat or tilting your head sideways (while wearing glasses) to achieve optimal polarization.

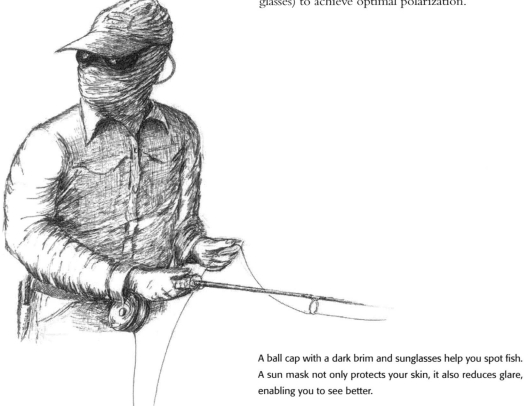

A ball cap with a dark brim and sunglasses help you spot fish. A sun mask not only protects your skin, it also reduces glare, enabling you to see better.

The Naked Truth about Spots

I have no closer friend than Pat Fulford, but I still didn't tell him about my secret spot in Mosquito Lagoon. But, he eventually found it on his own.

We preferred to fish separately, and two boats working closely together started to draw attention. Some folks find it easier to look for other boats fishing rather than wasting time looking for fish, and they came in from every direction to see what was cooking.

We came up with some grand schemes to deter the intruders. We scattered diving flags around, but boats just ran over them. Fulford's skiff was gray. I wanted to paint "Marine Patrol" on the hull and mount a blue light on top of the platform. Pat, a lawyer, said no. Even resting an engine cowling on top of the poling platform had no effect. We figured all but the good Samaritans would steer clear from towing a boat in distress back to the dock. They were nicer than us in that regard.

"What do you think they're fishing for?" one would inquire over the drone of the outboard as the anglers idled in. Sound carries well over water.

"Who cares?" the other replied, "Let's see if we can catch one!"

It was always comical to listen to them, but when they motored within casting range, things heated up fast. One day, a pair of trespassers got so close we could have cast across their deck. The normal boat banter and name calling ensued, and they finally asked, "What, do you think you own the water?" Then, they did the anchor toss thing. Some clowns can throw them so far and make such a big splash, you'd think it was an Olympic sport.

Their boat came to rest no more than 50 feet away. Nothing else seemed worth saying. Nothing I had ever said before had ever made a difference. Then, an idea flashed in my brain like a bolt of lightning. With the trespassers looking on, I ripped off all my clothes, jumped in the water, and swam toward them, yelling, "I'm naked as a jay bird!" Boy, did that work. After they quickly pulled anchor and left, Fulford and I laughed for the next hour. But obviously, things were getting out of hand.

That winter I had a heart attack, and the next summer I showed up at the "secret spot" with a softer, more live-and-let-live attitude. One day, I spotted a boat heading full bore directly at me. I measured my response, "Be nice . . . stay dressed . . . they know not what they do!" As the boat passed, I struggled to maintain my temper, and my balance, in its wake, and all I could do was shrug my shoulders in disbelief. Honest, that's all I did. It felt strange but also sort of good. There was a man at the helm with a small boy on board. No sooner had the boat passed me, it spun around and idled back just off my bow.

"You got some sort of problem fellow?" the man seemed to demand.

I couldn't believe it. My first attempt to be nice and this guy wants to start a fight.

As I came unglued and launched into a tirade, the man and boy just stared at me in disbelief.

Out of nowhere, the man responded, "Look mister, my son and I thought you were broken down. Do you need some help or not?"

Embarrassed, I tried to explain my behavior, but finally said, "Obviously I got a problem, but my motor's fine."

For the most part, I am over getting angry at other boaters. Jet skis still push my buttons from time to time, but in sixty years I've never managed to change anyone by yelling at them. Pogo was right, the enemy is us.

Body Language

A tarpon's body movements will not only help you figure out the best presentation, but also whether she is happy and feeding or not worth casting to. We've talked about laid-up fish, most common in the backcountry, and traveling fish, most common on the beach. Other tarpon behaviors such as rolling, free jumping, or busting can help you locate them, and by reading the fish's behavior, you can figure out how to best catch them.

Rolling Fish

Tarpon roll to gulp air, in both the backcountry and the beach. Quite often the sound of a fish rolling seems to provoke another fish within hearing distance to do the same. Also, two fish swimming together will frequently roll within seconds of one another. This occurs too often to be coincidence. I am convinced tarpon sometimes roll in response to the sound of other fish rolling much the way we yawn after someone else yawns. Though it may sound off the wall, I've often wondered if I could entice tarpon to show by imitating the sound of rolling fish.

Calm days on the water are a welcome sight, since tarpon tend to roll less frequently in rough or choppy water. Perhaps this is due to wave action aerating the water and increasing the levels of oxygen, much like a bait-well aerator. Younger tarpon tend to roll more often than mature fish.

Slicks are prime places to look for rolling tarpon. Tarpon will actually roll in or on the edges of slick areas during a light wind, perhaps because they prefer to roll in calmer water. When water depths are relatively consistent in the backcountry, traveling tarpon stick close to the slicks running across relatively still flats.

I like to enter a fishing area with the sun at my back, so that I can see the reflection of the sun off of the tarpon's silver sides as they roll. I stand on the bow (or poling platform if handling the boat) and scan the area, looking from side to side at varying distances for anything that captures my attention. Once I spot something of interest, and I know the water depth is OK for tarpon (for instance, not only a foot of water), I make a mental note of both angle and distance and focus there more frequently for longer periods. You might not see the actual fish from afar, but the duration of a typical tarpon's roll is distinguishable from diving water birds, dolphin, or turtles. I think of it like a flashbulb going off in the bleachers on the opposite side of a football stadium. You don't need to see the person holding the camera to know that was a flashbulb you saw.

Look for anything that interrupts the natural pattern of the water's surface, and keep an open mind as you scan the water. Don't look for the entire fish. A fish rolling away or straight ahead, the tip of a tarpon's tail descending between two waves, or sunlight glinting off a zigzagging dorsal fin are all clues.

Reading the Roll

A roll long, slow, and flat to the surface generally means the fish plans to stay near the surface as it moves ahead. Her tail and perhaps dorsal fin may stay visible for some distance. I usually grab my floating line rigged with the shorter leader, because in the low light, the long one is not necessary.

Tarpon that are going down roll in a much tighter arch, and the duration of the rolling period is much quicker. The top portion of the tail may become more vertical before disappearing below the surface. If I see this a lot, I'll choose a rod with a sinking-tip line, though if I am on the fence, I'll usually throw a floater, because that is what I prefer to use.

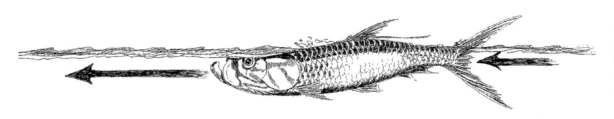

If the fish is rolling flat to the surface, it generally plans to stay there as it moves ahead. This fish is a prime target for a floating line and light fly.

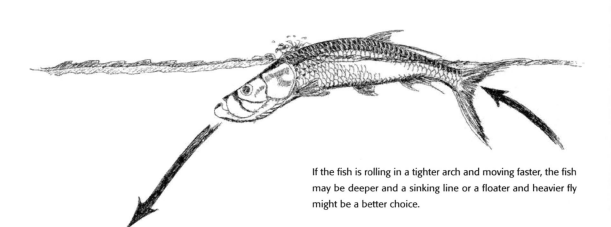

If the fish is rolling in a tighter arch and moving faster, the fish may be deeper and a sinking line or a floater and heavier fly might be a better choice.

When a tarpon rolls close by there are some split-second decisions to make:

1). Is the target in range? Just because you can make a long cast, doesn't mean that doing so is a good decision. Accuracy suffers with distance, and it is difficult to set a hook in the mouth of a tarpon at 80 feet because of the stretch in the fly line.

2). What is the angle, attitude, and speed of the fish? Is the fish coming straight at you or is she 90 degrees to the skiff? Was her roll flat or did she barrel roll toward the bottom? Asking these questions helps determine your presentation.

A fish 90 degrees to you is not optimal. Imagine you are looking at an intersection with one car approaching from the south and the other is coming from the west. The tarpon is one car and the fly is the other. Even though intersections are common places for wrecks, with only two cars in the equation, the odds of a collision are remote. You must not only lead the fish so that it meets your fly, but you have to guess where the fish is going, based on the premise it is traveling straight. Further complicating the issue, you must allow enough of a lead to compensate for the flight time of the fly and its sink rate, if she's still there at all.

An 80-foot cast to a rolling fish that's 90 degrees to you is a long shot, in more ways than one. Contrary to popular belief, those casters who cast the most don't usually hook up the most. Pass on low-percentage opportunities when there are a lot of rolling fish. Pick your targets patiently. The best casters can make the long shots, but they choose not to, often because it takes valuable fishing time to recover eighty feet of fly line, and you never know what will pop up closer to the boat. With all that said, when fish aren't showing well and opportunities are more limited, take every shot you can get.

A fish dead ahead at 40 feet, rolling flat and slow, is a higher percentage shot. The play on this target is simple. Don't overshoot the fish! Allowing for the time it takes for one backcast and the fly to settle in the water, throw 20 feet or so ahead. Remember that tiny intersection you were trying to

squeeze your fly into with that 90-degree fish? There is no intersection when dealing with a head-on target. You're both traveling in the same direction, in the same lane of traffic. All you've got to do is slow down and hope for a collision.

Daisy-Chaining Fish

A daisy chain is a group of fish (a few or many) following one another in a tight circle in either a clockwise or counterclockwise direction. Tarpon that chain on the surface are generally happy, undisturbed fish and are a tarpon angler's dream.

One day I asked Tommy Locke why he thought tarpon chained up so often. He laughed, "It might have something to do with mating, but most of the time I think a string of 'poons is swimming along when the guy in front decides to make a sharp turn. It's his or her parade. Everybody follows suit. Pretty soon the lead fish circles around and runs into the tail of the fish in the back of the line. The whole herd is caught in a merry-go-round until somebody realizes they're going nowhere and straightens things out."

Fish that tend to get my undivided attention are those that are in range, stay close to the surface, swim slowly, and offer the least amount of angle for presentation. The best of all this adds up to daisy-chaining fish (see illustration on page 15). They are on top and generally moving slowly. Because they are circling in one spot, you can feed several fish with one good cast and control the angle of your presentation by moving the boat.

Screw-Down Tarpon

When I first started fly fishing for tarpon, I would fish for a lot of screw-down tarpon. These fish spiral or screw down underneath the spot where they rolled and then release air bubbles. I suspect this exhaling of air allows them to reach a point of neutral buoyancy, because in most instances they lay up near the bottom.

Through trial and error, I figured out how to feed screw-down fish. The correct cast proved to

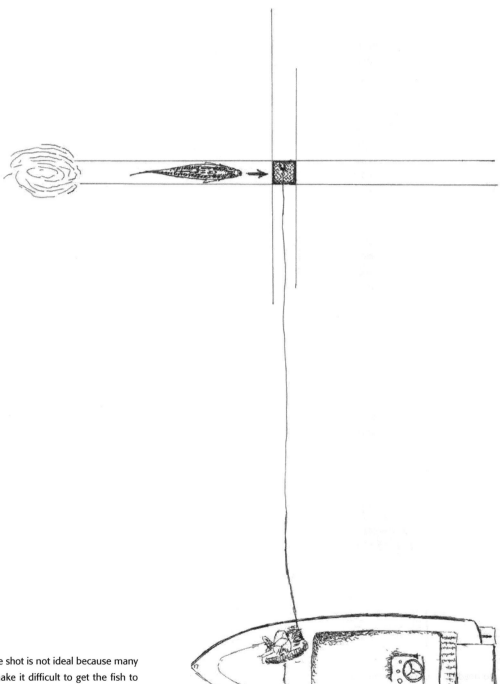

A 90-degree shot is not ideal because many variables make it difficult to get the fish to intercept the fly.

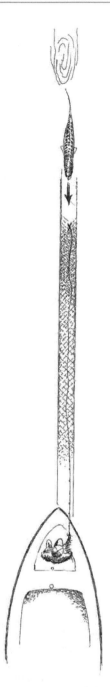

The head-on shot or one with a slight angle is best. The fly and the fish are traveling in the same lane.

be one where the fly landed 5 feet past and crossed over the bubbles on the surface. If the bubbles came straight up, the fish was holding. If the bubbles were trailing out in a line, the fish was swimming. Since the speed of the bubbles revealed the exact speed and direction of the fish, determining how far to lead the fish was easy. The bubbles told me the location of the mouth—I was pretty sure they weren't farting.

In either situation, I had to compensate for the fly's sink rate. A little basic math helped. I was fishing in about 7 feet of water with a fly that sank at a foot per second. I estimated the head of the fish to be about 2 feet off the bottom given the lush bed of grass that covered the area. I dove down and measured it. Tarpon rest with their heads down at about a 30-degree angle. This meant if I allowed the fly to sink 4 feet before stripping, it would be a foot or so above and 5 feet past the fish. Following a four-second countdown, I began a slow strip to bring the fly through the zone where a fish was most likely to respond. Sometimes I would have to work the fly right up to the boat before the fish ate.

Busting

Tarpon most often bust because something startles them. This can be as simple as a fish in the string being bumped by another or the presence of a bull or hammerhead shark in the area, which puts fish in a spooky mood. A single brown pelican gliding inches above the slick surface of a quiet bay is an everyday sight that often goes unnoticed by anglers. But the shadows of low-flying birds whizzing over their heads often spook tarpon, and I've seen the same bird cause several fish to bust on many occasions. A flock of pelicans is better yet. They fly in an offset and staggered formation rather than single file, thus covering more water.

Free-jumping fish are different than busting fish. I get the impression these fish are doing this for fun. There is no event that I know of that causes fish to free jump, but it's a surefire way to find them.

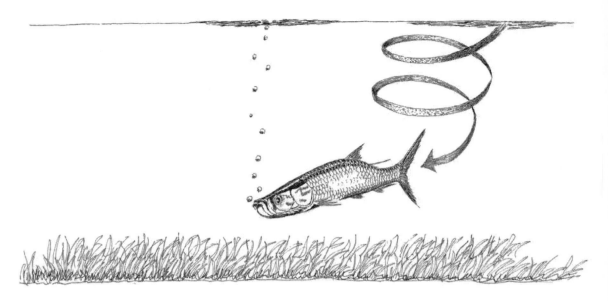

If bubbles come straight up, the fish is holding; if they are trailing out in a line, the fish is swimming.

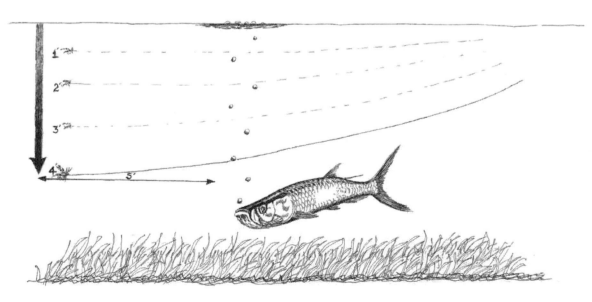

When fishing for screw-down tarpon, you need to compensate for the fly's sink rate.

Happy Fish

Finding tarpon isn't really all that tough. Most days you can go to Boca Grande Pass or motor along the beach, and you'll have no problem locating fish by spotting boats concentrated in tight groups. Tarpon are generally sulking along the bottom and trying to dodge the barrage of baits being lobbed on their heads. You'll even see fly anglers chasing the fleeing fish with their outboards and wildly casting in hopes of getting hooked up. Yes, there's tarpon there. Yes, tarpon eat flies. But you won't see many fish hooked.

Eating comes second to survival for tarpon, and when those once-happy, slow-moving fish that were once finned out on the surface pick up speed and sink to the bottom, the game is over until they settle down and regroup.

Our sport is becoming more and more challenging with every passing season given the number of anglers, pleasure boaters, and jet-ski enthusiasts. This isn't unique to Boca Grande. It's the same in the Keys and Homosassa. Because these folks have as much right to enjoy the re-sources as we do, you must strategize to find happy fish. Don't plan tarpon trips around holidays, and as a rule, weekdays are better than weekends. Get an early start and plan to fish late. Most recreational boaters don't get cranked up until midmorning. Since they break for lunch, midday is less crowded. Late-afternoon lightning storms send the crowds scurrying for the boat ramps, and a hard west sea breeze makes most pleasure boaters uncomfortable on the beach.

An airborne tarpon or two can attract attention from other anglers from astonishing distances and active tarpon grounds can get crowded. This is especially true when fishing along the beaches or any wide open water. I've seen it so crowded you couldn't cuss a cat without winding up with a mouth full of fur. When conditions get like this, I move on to another more peaceful and productive place. When fish are spooked and not eating, you should not waste your time trying to force feed them the fly. Move to find fresh fish. Recreational anglers have a slight advantage over professional guides when it comes to locating undisturbed fish.

Tarpon often bust because something startles them, such as brown pelicans flying low overhead.

Even when tarpon aren't chewing all that well, it's difficult for a guide with an anxious client to pull off fish and search for different ones.

In Boca Grande, and I expect in other fisheries, there is a three-day cycle that occurs once concentrations of fish show up. The first day is almost always the most productive. If you are fortunate enough to be one of the first on the scene, the action can be hot and heavy. The second day is less so due to the stress placed on the fish the day before and increasing pressure from more anglers who heard the fishing is good. By day three, it's normally all over. Only by having the discipline to venture out will you ever be the first on the scene at the next hot spot loaded with fresh happy fish. When this occurs, I usually call one of my guide friends and return the favor he did for me the week before. The disposition of most fishing guides won't allow them to express much in the way of appreciation, but if you were looking for that you would have called your mother.

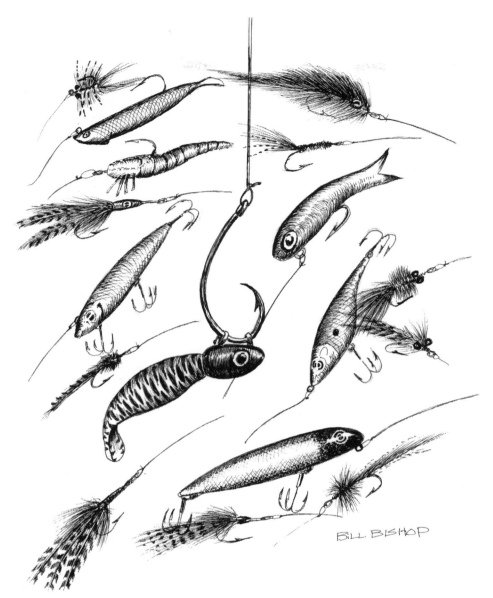

BILL BISHOP

Something Is Out of Place. In this illustration, you'll find 15 artificial baits and only one fish snagging device. In September 2013 the Florida Fish and Wildlife Conservation Commission unanimously passed the draft rule prohibiting the use of bottom-weighted jigs in Boca Grande Pass. This one decision eliminated the practice of snatch hooking tarpon. The vote, led by commission chairman Ken Wright, correctly concluded the bottom-weighted jig did not entice the fish to bite. Instead, by its very design, it snagged tarpon when fished vertically in the depths of the pass.

Enticing a fish to strike lies at the very core of honest angling. The key word here is *honest*. Bypassing this critical step turns fishing into just catching and totally eliminates the skill factor. In addition, the commission adopted new rulings that anglers are now allowed to harvest only one tarpon by purchasing a $50 harvest tag. This can only be used when in pursuit of an IGFA record fish. Lastly, all tarpon in excess of 40 inches must remain in the water during the process of release thus minimizing the useless killing of tarpon for photographic purposes.

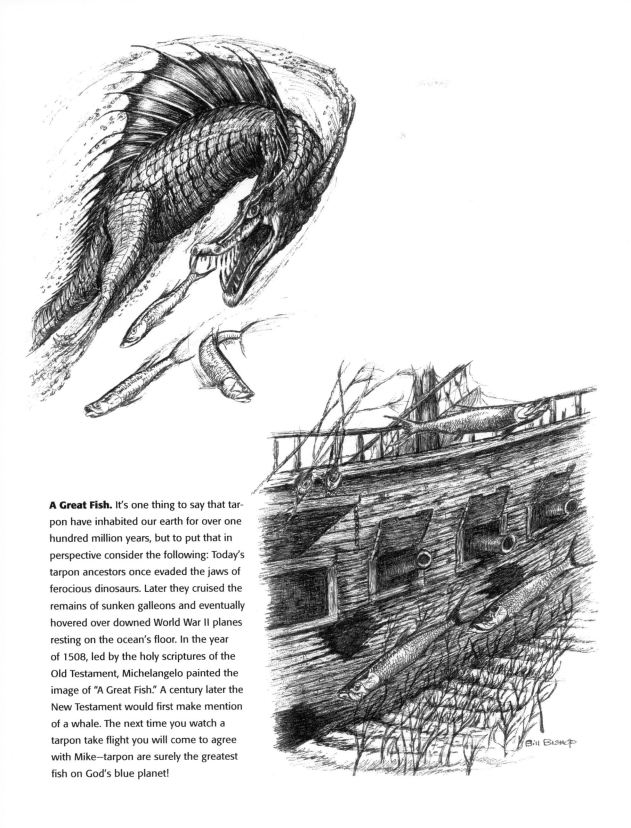

A Great Fish. It's one thing to say that tarpon have inhabited our earth for over one hundred million years, but to put that in perspective consider the following: Today's tarpon ancestors once evaded the jaws of ferocious dinosaurs. Later they cruised the remains of sunken galleons and eventually hovered over downed World War II planes resting on the ocean's floor. In the year of 1508, led by the holy scriptures of the Old Testament, Michelangelo painted the image of "A Great Fish." A century later the New Testament would first make mention of a whale. The next time you watch a tarpon take flight you will come to agree with Mike—tarpon are surely the greatest fish on God's blue planet!

The Silver River. The tarpon migration from Mexico through the Florida straits is a sight to behold. Each spring, posted sentinels, perched high upon their casting platforms, scan the horizon for the arrival of the silver river of tarpon. More often than not, one starry, moonlit night, riding high on the incoming tide, legions of silver king slide in. To the most hardcore tarpon anglers in the Florida Keys, the following morning is likened to the Fourth of July, Easter Sunday, and Christmas morning all wrapped up in a glistening chrome-plated package. The migration has arrived, and another tarpon season is upon us.

The Shadow. The presence of sharks along Florida's west coast, particularly hammerheads and bulls, have a profound effect on tarpon. With the arrival of the man in the grey suit, tarpon tend to sink lower in the water column and hug the bottom in their travels. Perfect fly presentations are most often refused during this time. An observant angler can recognize this behavior, and it typically isn't long before the culprit is spotted. They often follow the scent of the strings of fish moving along the drop-offs of the contour bars. Veteran anglers and guides know it's time to relocate to a new area.

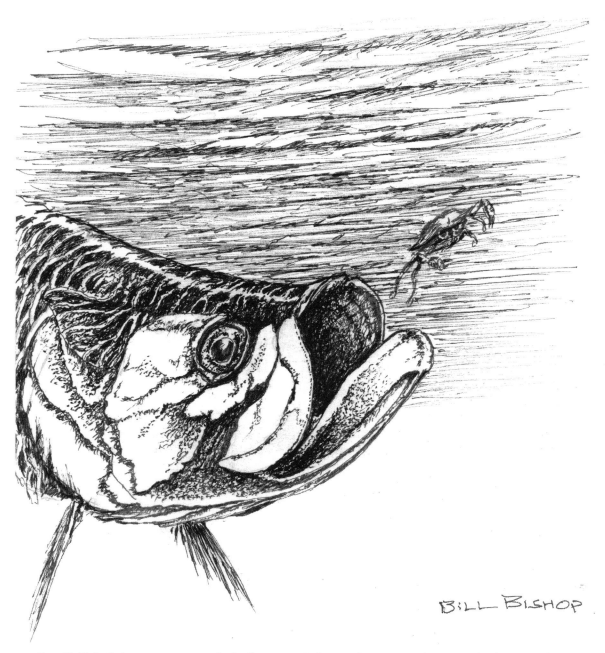

BILL BISHOP

Easy Pickin's. Crabs are an easy target for feeding tarpon. At times, crab patterns can be very productive. Less action should be imparted to the fly. Crabs floating along with the tide are often "sipped" by tarpon without fanfare. I've also witnessed this same behavior during the late summer seahorse hatches along the beaches on the west coast.

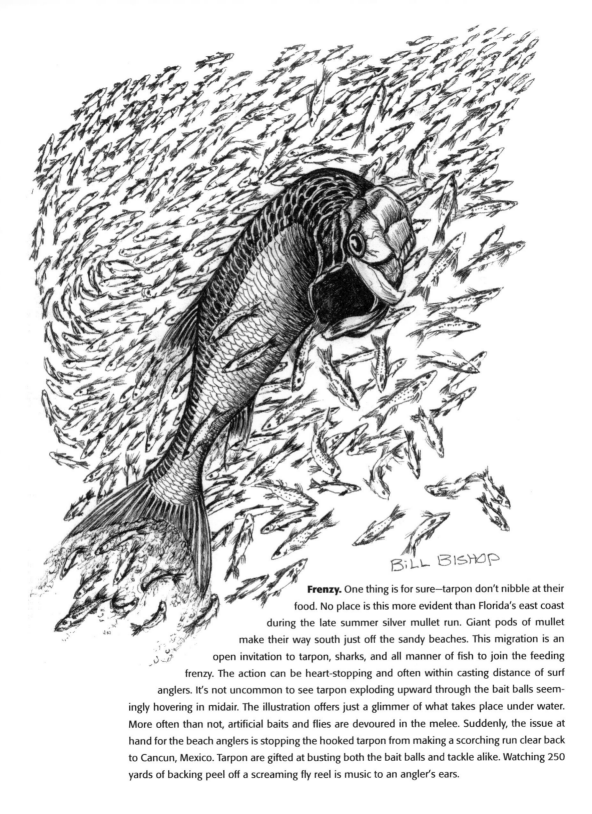

BILL BISHOP

Frenzy. One thing is for sure—tarpon don't nibble at their food. No place is this more evident than Florida's east coast during the late summer silver mullet run. Giant pods of mullet make their way south just off the sandy beaches. This migration is an open invitation to tarpon, sharks, and all manner of fish to join the feeding frenzy. The action can be heart-stopping and often within casting distance of surf anglers. It's not uncommon to see tarpon exploding upward through the bait balls seemingly hovering in midair. The illustration offers just a glimmer of what takes place under water. More often than not, artificial baits and flies are devoured in the melee. Suddenly, the issue at hand for the beach anglers is stopping the hooked tarpon from making a scorching run clear back to Cancun, Mexico. Tarpon are gifted at busting both the bait balls and tackle alike. Watching 250 yards of backing peel off a screaming fly reel is music to an angler's ears.

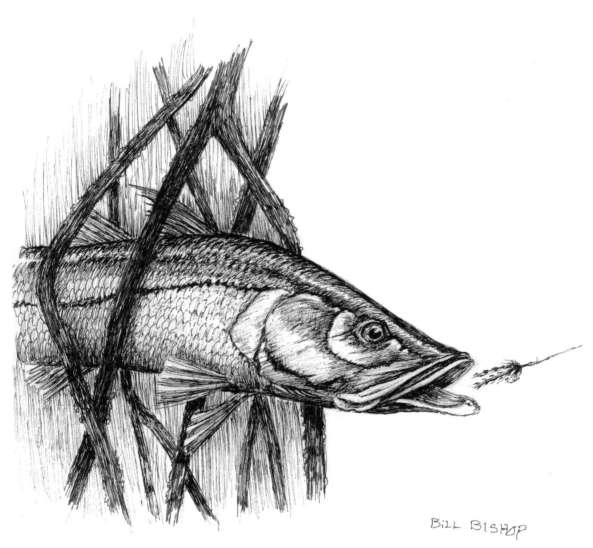

BILL BISHOP

Backcountry. Along the mangrove shorelines both snook and tarpon can be found. With the rising tide in the Everglades, tarpon tend to move closer to the shorelines. It's not uncommon for tarpon anglers to hear and see snook ambushing bait using the complex root structure as cover. Now and again, anglers are tempted to toss a tarpon fly in their direction. When snook are actively feeding they tend to ignore the heavier bite leaders and strike. It's safe to say, snook fishing is a close second to chasing tarpon. Like tarpon, they strike and fight with a vengeance. Unlike tarpon, they are excellent table fare.

Staying in the Game

When your partner or guide scrambles up on top of the poling platform and you take your position on the bow, you each have separate responsibilities that when properly shuffled together create the potential for a fish-catching machine. How do you hold up your part of the team?

Be Alert

The guide's primary job is locating fish and calling the shots. As a rule, the guide on the poling platform will see the fish before the angler due to his elevated position and experience. The angler's task is to respond quickly and accurately; therefore, he should not sit down or relax. For reasons that escape me, I see this a great deal. It's paramount to the pilot taking a nap while the navigator frantically calls out new course headings. Anglers who do this miss out on the enjoyment of the hunt and, more importantly, they may miss shots at fish.

Manage the Fly Line

A critical part of staying ready involves managing the fly line. You should stretch the fly line so it is straight and reverse the coils stacked on the deck. If you do not do this, the line coming off the deck first will be yanked from the bottom of the stack. This won't work. You wouldn't unravel a garden hose this way.

You can stretch and reverse the line together. Strip out the amount of line you are comfortable casting. Grasp the line closest to the reel and bring it taut between your two hands in about 3-foot sections. Pull your hands apart while firmly gripping the line, and stretch. Repeat this until you've stretched all the line. Some anglers place their foot on the line and pull upward on both sides of the line to straighten longer sections at a time. Allow the straightened line to coil in another spot on the deck, making sure when you've finished that the line leading from the uppermost coil goes through

Line properly coiled on the deck and an angler ready to cast. Be sure there is ample slack between the reel and the coils below.

your left hand (if you're right-handed) and directly to the bottom rod guide. This becomes second nature in no time. Guard against disturbing the coiled line as much as possible.

Be mindful to provide ample slack between the reel and the coils below. Gain this slack from the reel spool instead of pulling it from the deck. Remember, this part of the line now leads to the bottom coil in the stack. If this is too taut, your casting motions can disturb the coils, resulting in a tangled mess.

I like to make large coils on the deck because they are less prone to tangling. Since I am right-handed, I coil the line on my left side and slightly

behind my feet. If standing on the forward deck, I coil the line on the floor of the boat, if possible, to keep it away from my shoes and out of the wind, which can wreak havoc with loose fly line. If a wave washes inside the cockpit or across the deck and disturbs the coils, regroup and start over.

If you leave your rod unattended, maintain it in a ready position by looping the fly line over the hook shank and insert the point in the cork handle. In addition to protecting the hook point, you can pick the rod up and cast your fly quickly. This method is a little tough on the cork, but staying ready is worth it.

Preparation

I check my class tippet for nicks or abrasions while looking for fish, sliding it slowly through my fingertips to feel for any damage. If I feel anything suspicious, I change flies. I also inspect the hook point by dragging it across my thumbnail. If it slips or slides, I sharpen it. I clean my sunglasses a dozen times a day. I am mindful of anything that might snag fly line. Tackle bags, rain jackets, leader stretchers, and towels are notorious for winding up in the wrong place on a skiff. Fly fishermen are busy bodies indeed.

I wear pliers so I don't have to search for them when unhooking a fish, and I wear them on my right side, opposite the side that I strip my fly line. I keep fully rigged and sharpened flies stored in leader stretchers stowed nearby should I get a refusal and need to switch to an alternate color or pattern. Also stored within easy reach is a small watertight bag containing a measuring tape, camera, tarpon tag, and calculator for determining the weight of a potential record tarpon. Lastly, when fishing alone, I keep my outboard positioned straight so I can take chase without hesitation, but with the prop just below the water's surface so it doesn't cause too much drag while working my electric motor or poling.

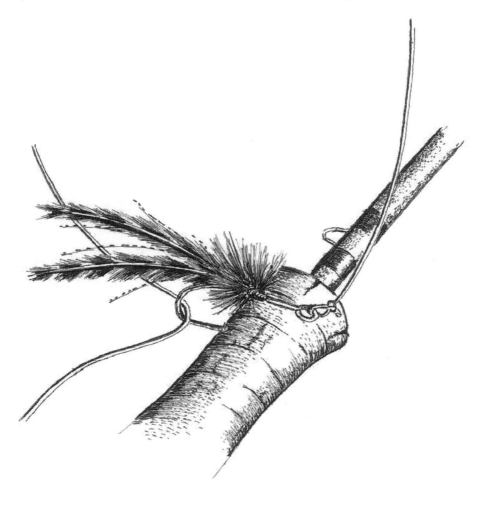

Tarpon have no appointments and they don't mind getting wet.

Optimism

Preparation is not enough to catch fish on a regular basis. Only one or two skiffs on the tarpon flats consistently have tarpon dancing off their bows, even though all the other anglers may be doing each of the mechanical aspects correctly. Sooner or later luck runs out, but these few anglers are still jumping fish. What's the difference?

Optimism.

Do tarpon know the mindset of the person on the other end of the line? No. But they know the difference between a half-hearted fly presentation and a first-class selling job. Thirty years in retail sales taught me that an optimistic attitude is an outward expression of an inner confidence that can often make the difference between winning and losing. Trust me. One of the most delicate selling jobs on earth is feeding a 3-inch fly to a 6-foot tarpon.

Tarpon have no appointments, and they couldn't give a hoot how long you have been staked out on the edge of a bar. Like a blue heron patiently poised on a shoreline waiting for dinner to swim by, you may need to stand there through both tides before the fish show up—if they do at all.

And, they may show up the minute you pull off, when you look away to get a drink of water, or when you go to the bathroom.

Tarpon seem to show up so frequently when you are pulling away that Charlie Madden and I have invented the "deek," which is slang for decoy. The art of deeking takes years of practice, and I must say, Charlie and I may be two of the best. Here's how it goes. After several hours with no action, one angler shouts to the other, "Let's get out of here . . . there's no fish coming." The other responds, "You bet, let's go!" Now a full-fledged

Rough seas, pitching decks, extreme heat, casting heavy rods, and doing battle with fish that weigh a hundred pounds can test your physical conditioning.

deek can go all the way to actually pulling anchors and firing up the engines. All the while neither of us has the slightest intention of going anywhere. More often than not, the fish appear shortly after. If not, we pull anchors and move on. Blind optimism, different from the other kind of optimism, doesn't sink to the depths of pessimism, but it straddles the fence on being stupid. Finding a better place to spend our time and energy once a full-fledged deek has been attempted is just plain common sense. After all, there's other fish in the sea.

Pace

When I first arrive at our home in Boca Grande, I seem to always be in a dither to rush out on the water. Typically I don't fish well until I take a deep breath and stop running about like a sprayed cockroach. This pace doesn't lend itself to correctly making the countless sound decisions needed to ensure a fun, safe, and successful trip on the water. Once I settle down, things tend to fall in line, and I can enjoy being on the water. Some folks never get there. They seem to never be satisfied where they are until they've run 15 miles down the beach and back just to see if they were missing something. I don't know how much fuel they carry, but it must be a bigger tank than mine.

Physical Conditioning

Fly fishing for tarpon requires athleticism. Rough seas, pitching decks, extreme heat, casting heavy rods, and doing battle with fish that weigh a hundred pounds can test your physical conditioning. Some anglers that stand up from their desk and go immediately to the bow of a tarpon skiff suffer needlessly, and their performance suffers as well. Yes, getting your equipment and gear in shape is important, but don't forget your body is the engine that drives all this expensive gear.

Dr. Chris Broulliette is a fine physician and a superb tarpon angler and offers this advice to anglers who take their fly fishing seriously: "In addition to muscle conditioning, balance is also critical. You're trying to throw a fly to a moving target from a moving platform. Balance is a matter of the various muscle groups receiving messages from the brain. It's not necessarily related to strength, but has more to do with the muscles working together with the brain to stay upright and under control. As we grow older, we tend to engage less in activities that require balance, and our reaction time suffers. Stay involved in activities that require you to react."

CHAPTER TEN

Casting

I grew up convinced cussing profusely was a necessary step in the art of casting. Dad loved plugging for trout, snook, and redfish, and I can still hear his Penn 109 whine as tan linen line peeled off the spool, sending a yellow Zara Spook sailing toward the white sand holes in the lush eel-grass flats. The backlashes that reel would produce were nothing short of mind-boggling.

Though I have now graduated to more sophisticated and expensive tackle, not much has changed, because there is still plenty of cussing when casting to fish. While we do not have to contend with backlashes, there are still tangles, snags, lines that won't shoot, and hooks stuck in body parts—and that's not even taking into account all the cussing I hear on the flats from my pals who overshoot fish, or undershoot them, or their line just plain piles up 20 feet short because of the 20-mile-an-hour headwind.

Casting is one of the challenges of our sport, and we all have our good days and bad, but it is easier to learn than feeding, hooking, or fighting fish. Perhaps this is because you don't need a tarpon in front of you to become a good caster. You can learn to cast through good instruction and by lots of practice in your own backyard. On the other hand, the other skills require considerable bow time and the assistance of willing tarpon. They are prolific, but they don't grow on trees. Having said all of that, casting will probably seem like your greatest challenge at the beginning.

A fly rod is not a way of making the sport more difficult or challenging. The fly rod is the most effective fishing tool you will ever hold in your hand. It will deliver an artificial offering with more grace and less disturbance than any outfit you presently own. In the time you can make two casts to a tailing fish with spinning gear, you can easily make three with a fly rod. Once you hook the fish with a fly rod, you can beat it faster, with less effort, and with more enjoyment.

Most saltwater anglers become accustomed to casting 7- to 9-weight rods for smaller fish such as redfish or snook before taking on larger tackle. An 11- or 12-weight seems huge at first, but that rod shrinks considerably when a 130-pound tarpon is charging your fly less than 30 feet off the bow. Heavier rods are not designed as fine fly-casting

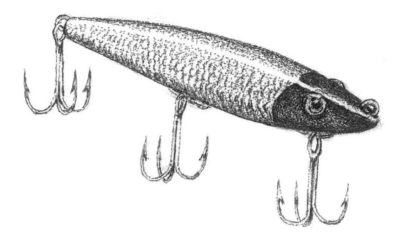

tools. They are designed for fighting fish and are nothing more than a fly delivery system. With that said, the tarpon rods available today cast very well and are relatively light compared with the tarpon rods we had ten years ago.

I won't even attempt to stumble my way through the fine points of fly casting. Experts have created many great books and videos on this subject. The best of these, in my opinion, feature Lefty Kreh's wisdom. I do, however, have a few pieces of advice.

Learn to make a 90-foot forward cast with no more than two or three backcasts. To do this, you will need to learn how to double haul. There is more to casting than just distance. Learn how to cast without a lot of body movement, which can rock the boat. Fish feel the waves with their lateral lines and shy away.

All guides will tell you their most common problem has nothing to do with finding fish. They are on the water daily and know where the fish are. The real challenge is finding good casters who can deliver flies to fish in a reasonable amount of time with a minimum amount of commotion. Anglers should know how to cast before stepping up on the bow of a skiff. You owe yourself and the guide that much. Many anglers find their high expectations before a trip are shattered by their inability to

cast. Most fly guides will quiz potential clients regarding their casting ability. If you can cast he will be enthusiastic beyond your expectations, and he will work hard until dark to get you shots. If you can't, he won't say a word. He will be in it only for his daily rate and a tip. Odds are it's going to be an expensive and gut-wrenching day for both of you.

If you can't cast effectively, consider putting off your trip until you've practiced enough so that you can. You will be doing yourself a favor. I live two blocks from a golf country club where I am a member. This past fall, almost every time I attempted to go to the practice range, there were a dozen folks there practicing their swings and shots with various clubs. They don't call it the practice range for nothing. If fly casters practiced as much as golfers, casting woes wouldn't be the number one reason most folks don't hook up with tarpon.

In addition to the basic casts and learning how to double haul; a curve cast, underhand cast, roll cast, and backhand cast can come in handy.

Curve Cast

Years ago, I had the privilege of spending four days with Lefty Kreh. I had fished with Lefty before this particular trip, but this time our mission involved work. I was illustrating a book he was writing about casting in salt water, and Lefty was emphatic that I learn how to make every cast. I was more than willing to learn from the master.

Even though I learned how to make a curve cast, I was certain I would never really put it to use in my tarpon fishing. I didn't let on to Lefty what I thought. I ain't the brightest guy around, but I'm not stupid either. I envisioned the curve cast to be suitable for guiding a fly around pilings and such, but that was about it.

The following summer, I found myself in a challenging and frustrating situation. I was posted on the edge of a bar that jutted straight out from a narrow pass. The hard incoming tide swept past my skiff and straight down the edge of the drop

off where string after string of tarpon politely refused my fly, which I was working against the flow. It was late in the afternoon, and the sun was squarely to my back. Any attempt to reposition the boat disabled my ability to see the incoming fish due to glare.

I was keenly aware of the problem but clueless as to the solution. To this day, I don't know what made me think of trying a curve cast, but I gave it a shot. Just as Lefty had instructed, I lowered the rod parallel to the water and picked out a spot well to the right of the lead fish. I replayed his instruction in my mind: "The fly goes in the direction of the speed up and stop." In a perfect curve the fly landed 5 feet ahead of the lead fish and

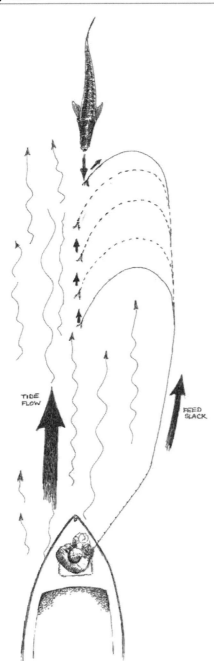

Sometimes you have to get creative. A curve cast saved the day in this situation. It is important to work your fly with the flow of current and away from the fish.

continued heading down current as I fed line from the deck. It would have gone that way until I ran out of fly line, but the tarpon inhaled it.

I was beside myself when I got to the house and called Lefty. I recounted my experience and creativity. He chuckled, "Why do you think I taught you how to make that cast? Trout guys have been using that since the beginning of time!"

Underhand Cast

An overhand cast naturally sends the fly down toward the water. Tarpon, like most fish, don't like things crashing down on top of their heads. Their awareness of this is keener in clear water or slick calm conditions. Despite their size, they can still shy away from a fly, leader, or fly line.

When conditions are slick and fish are on top and spooky, I often use a cast that stays very low to the surface of the water. This is because the rod tip stays close to the water on the forward cast and the fly passes under the rod tip instead of over the top. Lefty taught me this some years ago while we were standing on my dock in Mosquito Lagoon. The purpose of the cast was to send the fly so low to the water that it skips on the water and travels under things like mangroves and docks.

The cast I use also brings the fly in almost horizontal to the surface of the water, but it doesn't skip. If you use too much force, the fly rises up at the end of the cast, which is not ideal. Use just enough force on the forward cast to get the leader to straighten out, and the fly will actually enter the water tail first, making for an extremely soft landing.

Roll Cast

Roll casts are necessary when fishing sinking lines. Before beginning your backcast to lift the line out of the water, you need to make sure that sinking line is on the surface by using a roll cast. This is not a cast most anglers associate with tarpon fishing with floating lines, but it can be effective for repositioning the fly back in a string or higher in the water column without taking the time, motion, and effort to perform a backcast. If there is a break in the string, you can often make this cast without being detected by the fish. I have also used a short roll cast on laid-up fish.

Backhand Cast

It hurts when you drive a hook in your leg, but hooking the guy on the poling platform could be far more detrimental to your health. To prevent this use a backhand cast when the wind is blowing the fly line and the fly back toward you or the guide on the platform. For example, if you are right-handed, you will be at risk of hooking yourself when a stiff wind is coming from your right-hand side. You can beat the wind by turning and facing the opposite direction and releasing the fly on the backcast rather than the forward cast.

Getting Stuck

The number one thing an angler can bring on a tarpon trip is the ability to cast. All the fancy clothes, sunglasses, and fly-fishing gear can't make up for this one simple fact. Being able to listen and following instructions is second.

Tommy Locke and I have been friends for twenty years. Tommy is the best tarpon guide I know. Each year Tommy and I spend five days or so fishing for the elusive 200-pound fish on 16-pound-test in Homosassa. We've done this for years. We have come close to landing one, but thus far no cigar.

Tommy has had much to do with my involvement in this sport. His instruction over the years on casting, feeding, hooking, and fighting tarpon has proven invaluable. Even though I spend several hundred days each season fishing alone, I take full advantage of Tommy's expertise when he is on the platform. I cast when and where he says.

One summer, the fish didn't show in Homosassa, so we fished Boca Grande instead. It was loaded. At first light, we found long strings of fish pouring down a bar in Pine Island Sound. Tommy was poling into a 10-knot southeast wind when a huge fish rolled 60 feet to the right. "Hit him," he instructed.

A backhanded cast was my only chance. I hooked Tommy in the back years ago trying to bring the fly between us, and as big and tough as he is, I think one time might be my limit. I knew all too well the wind would be pushing the fly back toward me, but I thought I could pull it off. No dice. With a thud, the #3/0 Mustad 34007 SS buried up and under my left knee cap, well past the hook bend. To make matters worse, it had center-punched the large tendon running along the outside of my knee.

Tommy grabbed a length of leader material, confident he could dislodge the fly by wrapping the monofilament around the hook bend and pulling. When he looked at the pulsating tendon, he said, "We've got to get you to a hospital."

I had no plans on going to a hospital, but I sure wanted the fly out of my leg. "There's got to be another way," I exclaimed.

Tommy called a fellow guide 5 miles away. He had two doctors on board. Each bow slap from the head-on chop was excruciatingly painful. "What kind of doctors are they?" I yelled over the whine of the outboard.

Tommy grinned, "I think he said veterinarians!"

We pulled alongside their boat. The younger of the two orthopedic surgeons climbed aboard and surveyed the situation. "The hook has penetrated the tendon and is well embedded in the interior of the knee cap," he said grimly.

"Pull it out?" I begged.

"I can't guarantee the tendon won't be damaged," he warned.

Handing him pliers from my belt, I said, "That'll be my problem, not yours."

He looked around the cockpit of the skiff.

"What are you looking for," asked Tommy from his platform perch.

The doc smiled, "Something for your pal here to hold on to."

I looked up just in time to see Tommy turn around and stick his fingers in his ears.

"I'll do it on the count of three," he said. I nodded sheepishly. He did it on two. The doc held up the fly, inspecting something white dangling from the hook point. "That's the sheath material from the tendon."

After thanking the doctor profusely, Tommy and I idled away. "You look a little pale. Can I get you something?"

I mustered a smile, "Scotch!"

Over the balance of that day and the next, we jumped twenty-eight tarpon. We might have jumped more, but I didn't have the guts to try another backhanded cast. Tommy spun the boat so many times on that trip, we both got dizzy.

Casting a fly rod is one of the most gratifying experiences on earth, but it can be detrimental to your health.

CHAPTER ELEVEN

Feeding Fish

Feeding tarpon, presenting your fly to the fish in an enticing manner, is an art that can take years to develop. You can accelerate the process if you are fishing in clear water and can observe how fish react to your flies and you have the right guide on the poling platform to help you grasp the concept of feeding fish. In my case, Tommy Locke taught me much of what I know on the subject. Most newcomers to this sport give little or no thought to feeding fish. I didn't. I thought stripping the fly was all there was to it.

Imagine you are sitting in a chair at the far end of a room. You are holding a stick with a length of string, stretched out straight across the floor, to which a feather is attached. A cat enters and starts slinking across the room. The cat doesn't notice the feather because it's still too far away and it's not moving. As the cat crosses the room, he approaches the spot where the feather is resting. You wait. Only when the cat is in the right zone, say 3 feet or so from the feather, do you move the feather. Be careful. Too much action may startle

the cat and too little will be unnoticed. A slight "bump" should do the trick.

What do you expect the cat to do? Is he going to pounce on the feather? No, not in most cases. The cat will stop, crouch, and eye the target. You've got the cat's attention. How do you know this? You watched the cat respond to the movement of the feather.

That's exactly what you are trying to do with the tarpon. Get his attention. Nothing more, nothing less. Watch the tarpon's response. Much like the cat, he will spread his pectoral fins and slow down, crouching if you will. It took me years to pick up on this, but tarpon can actually hinge their heads to look at a well-placed fly. It's almost humanlike. I don't know how they do this, but they do. Next, it will change course and begin to track the fly, sinking slightly below it. Gradually increase the speed of the bumps to imitate a retreating bait. Sounds simple, right? Not on your life.

I love fishing in clear water on bright, sunny days because of the visual aspect of feeding the fish

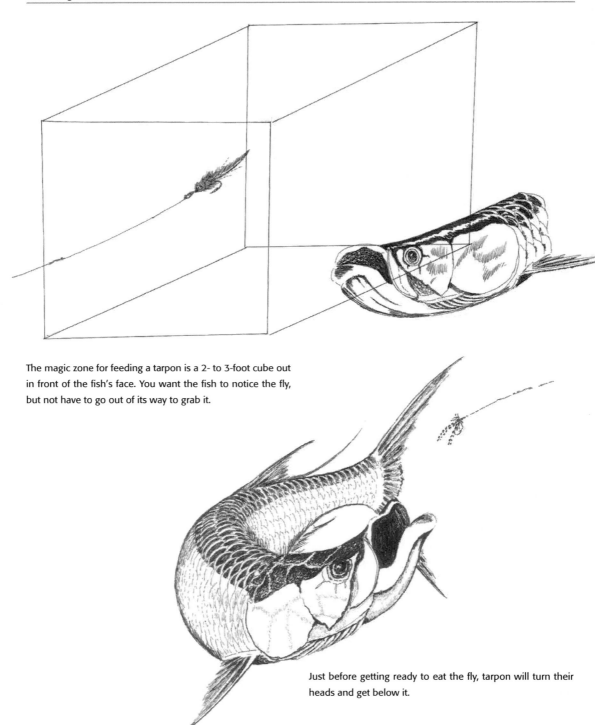

The magic zone for feeding a tarpon is a 2- to 3-foot cube out in front of the fish's face. You want the fish to notice the fly, but not have to go out of its way to grab it.

Just before getting ready to eat the fly, tarpon will turn their heads and get below it.

and watching its reactions and the take. Whether it's your first tarpon on fly or if you've jumped a million, when you feed a fish properly and you watch that 6-foot fish inhale the fly, your heart is pounding, your hands are shaking, and your legs feel like rubber.

Test the Water

Test your fly in the water. Make a cast or two before you start fishing. Take a mental note of the sink rate and the tide's effect on the fly and line. This will help later when you need to make split-second decisions.

The Clock

The guide usually sees the fish first (more experienced eyes and higher elevation on the platform) and points out the fish's position, most often by using the clock system. For example, the bow is 12 o'clock and 3 and 9 are directly out on opposite sides of the skiff. Unfortunately, this tells the angler nothing about distance, angle, or speed of the fish, so the guide should add information such as "75 feet, traveling slow" or another system.

If there is a delay before the angler picks up on the target and announces, "I've got 'em," I've found it helpful to glance at the back of the angler's hat to determine if he or see is looking in the right direction. Some guides will have the angler point the fly rod and direct its movements verbally from the platform or use their push pole as an extended finger toward the fish. The closer the fish, the louder some guides bark their whereabouts.

Identify the Lead Fish

As far as tarpon are concerned, there is no hierarchy that determines the first fish in the string. The only reason the lead fish is in front is that somebody has to be there. On the other hand, the lead

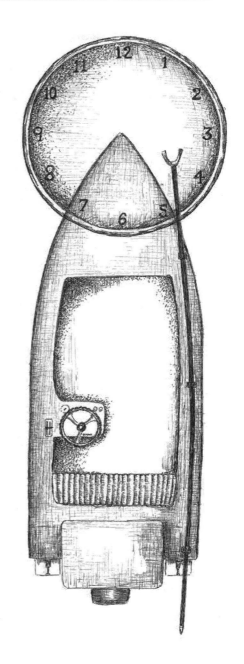

In the clock system, 12 o'clock is the bow, and 3 and 9 o'clock are perpendicular, on opposite sides of the skiff.

Though this 90-degree shot is a tough one, it was the only opportunity at the time. Generally, you should try and cast to the first fish in the string, called the lead fish. MARK HATTER PHOTO

fish is important to anglers. While these fish in the string are not in contact with one another, any event out of the norm is telegraphed down the line as if they were all wearing headsets. The angler must identify the lead fish so he can cast the fly ahead of the string so that the lead fish intercepts it. A cast that lands in the middle of the string or between two fish is rarely eaten and stands a good chance of spooking all the fish.

When you're watching for approaching fish, don't assume the first fish you see is the lead fish. The fish you spotted first may be higher in the water column and therefore more visible than the others. Keep scanning ahead of the fish you can

see until you are confident you have identified the lead fish in a string.

Time is of the essence when you are trying to identify the lead fish. First, the fish are getting closer. Second, your angle of presentation to the entire string of fish will be no better than your angle to the lead fish. If that's 90 degrees or more, you're not going to come out a winner.

Lead the Fish

You want to land your fly far enough ahead of the pack so that it doesn't spook the lead fish when it hits the water. Also, the fly needs time to settle and sink. In most cases about 8 to 10 feet should do the trick; however, if the water is clear or when dealing with spooky fish, I've stretched that out to 20 or 30 feet and had the best success with a longer leader. In stained or dirty water you can play it closer.

Tarpon often do not swim in a straight line. They meander. The lead fish sets the pace and dictates the direction of the string. Tarpon in a string have one single nervous system. If you spook the first fish, the rest of the fish will react accordingly. I have seen a few fish in the back of the line that didn't get the message, but that's rare.

Depth Is Critical

Many shallow-water anglers are only concerned about accuracy on a horizontal plain. Equally im-

portant is where the fly is positioned vertically in the water column. The sweet spot in the water column can vary from one species to another. For example, redfish and bonefish feed down. Their mouth is set well back under their nose. Tarpon prefer feeding up. This is because the lower jaw extends upward, and the eyes of a tarpon are mounted high on the front of her face. A fly that sinks below the face of an incoming tarpon will often go unnoticed.

The fly's sink rate dictates how far you can lead an approaching fish. You want it to be above its face when the fish encounters the fly. A fly riding high in the water column is best in this situation. Flies with a faster sink rate may be the ticket for some situations in the backcountry when fish are working deep. If I want a fly to sink faster but I like the pattern of one that won't, I wrap a few

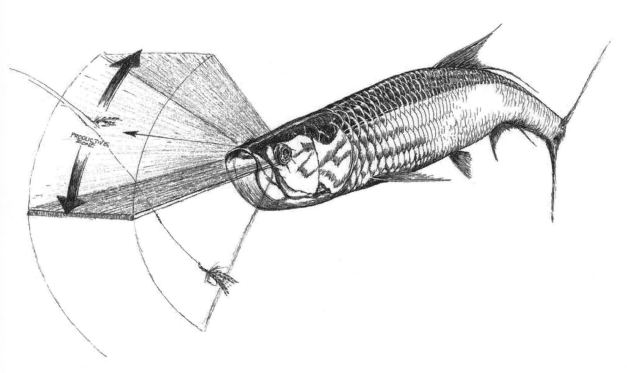

Tarpon prefer to feed up, so you are better off with the fly higher in the water column than below the fish.

turns of solder wire just behind the hook eye. Unlike lead or bead-chain eyes, the wire can be added or removed in seconds.

Wait for the Best Shot

A common mistake anglers make is to cast too early to approaching fish. Just because you can throw all the fly line, doesn't mean that you have to. Some reason that they might be able to squeeze in a second cast if they cast early, but the casts that follow the first one are usually not as effective. In most cases, one well-placed shot should seal the deal. As long as you have a good angle of presentation, you can wait until the fish are in close range.

Don't Overshoot Too Much

The second most common mistake is casting too far, common when adrenalin is flowing—especially with male casters. They get all puffed up, flex their muscles, and send the fly God knows where. My daughter, Shannon, doesn't have this problem. She simply puts the fly where it's supposed to go, most of the time. No fuss, no muss. I guess this only proves that a man should never be allowed to estimate the length of anything.

I will often cast a few feet beyond the lead fish just in case it turns out slightly, and slowly pull the fly into position. If you cast farther than a few feet, you may have to pull the fly quickly into position, which can startle the fish. If the lead fish shies off, the rest of the string follows. Also, correct fly placement is always on the side of the tarpon's face closest to you. If you cast too far, you risk working the fly toward the fish, and baitfish don't chase tarpon.

A few years ago, I watched from the poling platform as a good friend made one mistake after another when feeding fish. He was becoming frustrated. On one presentation, he cast past the fish and retrieved the fly toward the lead tarpon's face. The entire string bolted.

"What was wrong with that?" whined my buddy.

"The fly was chasing the tarpon."

"There's no way that big fish could be afraid of that little fly!" he protested.

I replied, "You're a pretty big guy . . . much bigger than that fish, right?"

He nodded.

"Imagine this," I continued, "You look out about 3 feet ahead of this skiff and a bumblebee, much smaller than a tarpon fly, is on a hostile vector straight for the tip of your nose. How are you going to react?"

He got it.

Target Practice

Once I was playing golf with longtime friend and seasoned golfer Kenny Hill. Kenny positioned himself behind me as I lined up my second shot on a par five. Just before I hit the ball, Kenny asked, "What's your target?"

I pointed down the fairway.

He laughed, "What are you aiming to hit?"

I laughed, "The golf course."

"Listen Bill, that's a lot like standing on the bow of your skiff while you watch incoming fish and your primary objective is to land your fly in the Gulf of Mexico!"

Anglers who can cast accurately reap the biggest rewards in this game. Instead of looking at the tarpon, I like to pick a spot on the water for my fly to land on and concentrate on hitting that. Practice casting to specific targets in your yard or from the deck of your skiff during slow periods. (Accuracy is easier from an anchored or posted skiff because you do not have to also compensate for the skiff's movement.) Pick out a moving leaf on the surface and lead it as if it were the tarpon's nose. During these practice sessions, you should be relaxed and focused only on the target you are trying to hit. Allow your natural eye-to-hand coordination to come into play and avoid overcalcu-

Correct. Fly positioned on the side of the tarpon's face closest to the angler.

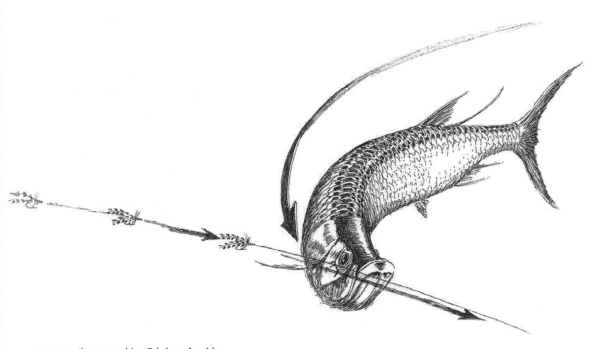

Incorrect. Fly approaching fish from far side

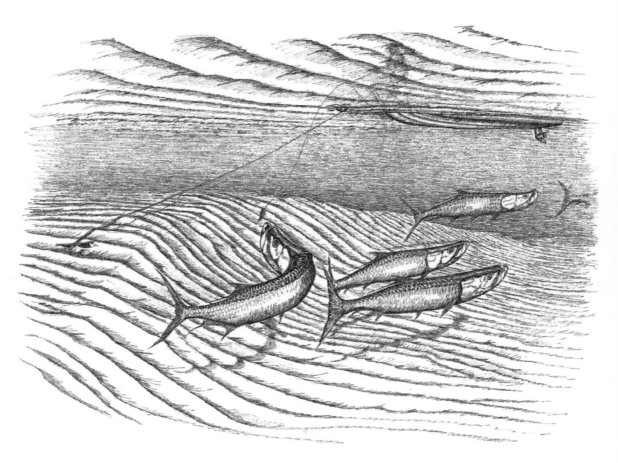

Feeding fish is all about angles. Ideally you should position the boat so that you can make a head-on or 20- to 45-degree cast and feed the entire string of fish.

lating the situation. Think of your cast as if you were casually tossing a wadded-up piece of paper in a nearby trash can.

Guides can play a huge part in helping or hampering your casting accuracy. If a guide can't remain calm and avoid yelling, trade him in for one that can. If you wanted pressure, you would have stayed at the office! Good guides remain calm and composed when directing their anglers to cast at specific targets in pressure situations.

All about Angles

The angle of your presentation is critical. With the exception of laid-up tarpon, fish facing away are not reasonable targets. Tarpon directly approaching you (from any direction) are head-on shots. Fish passing broadside to you are 90-degree targets. Then there is everything in between. Since you can't control the direction in which tarpon choose to swim, you must control the angle of your presentation by moving the skiff, either by posting up strategically or poling the boat into the best position.

Many anglers pray for the head-on shot in which the lead fish is swimming directly at them. I prefer a slight angle, which is far more forgiving and allows me to feed numerous fish in the string without being concerned that the lead fish is going to bump the skiff or be spooked by my rod movement. As the tide or the direction of the line of the fish changes, I move to maintain this angle. A simple adjustment of 5 to 10 feet can make the difference between success and failure. A 90-degree shot is my least favorite angle, because you are asking the fish to turn 90 degrees to eat the fly. The more effort you ask of the tarpon, the less likely it is to eat.

Unfortunately, other factors often come into play. Perhaps because of glare, wind direction, or strong seas, you are forced to present the fly from a

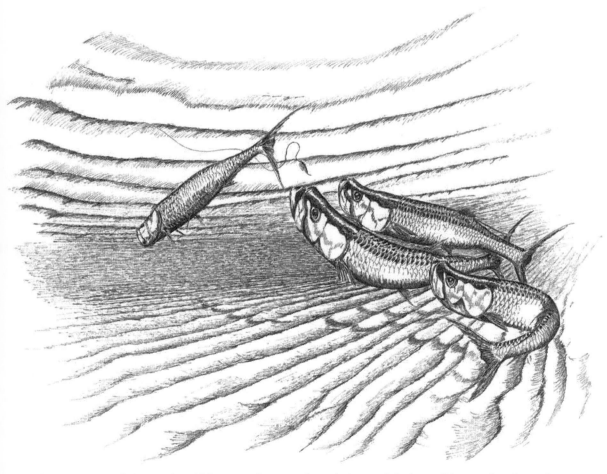

When you cast your fly into a string of fish, you can leave your fly motionless, until the largest fish comes into the magic zone. But, sometimes, something as simple as the tail wash from another fish brings the fly to life and ruins that plan.

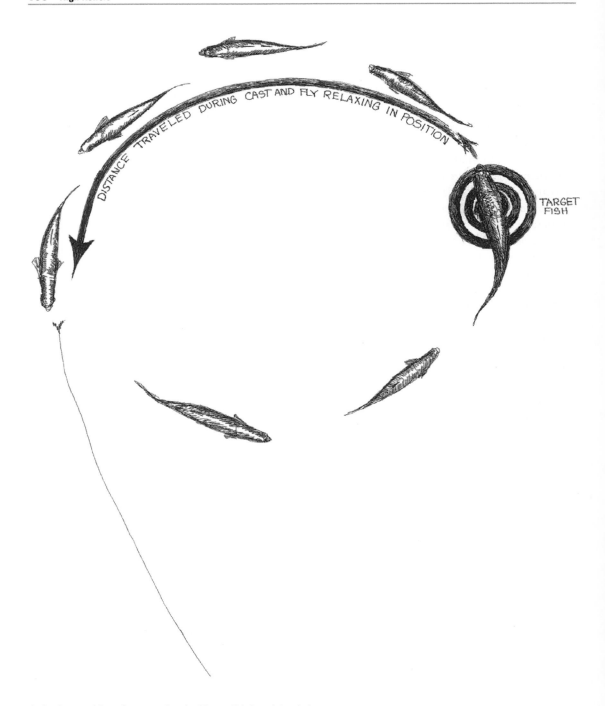

Timing is everything when targeting the biggest fish in a daisy chain.

less-than-ideal angle. Nonetheless, the boat handler should always be considering how to improve the caster's angle.

Calling the Shots

When most people book a guide to go tarpon fishing, they are content with catching any of the fish in a string. In most situations any fish will do. But when you are targeting trophy fish, you have to focus on feeding the largest ones.

The only reason I leave Boca Grande to fish Homosassa each season is to land the elusive 200-pound fish on 16-pound. I'm not alone in this endeavor. As a rule one can expect to see fewer fish in Homosassa than other fisheries, but the average size can be considerably larger. Tommy Locke and I aren't in Homosassa to rack up numbers of fish. If that were the case, we'd be back in our home waters. That's not to say fish this large can't be found in Boca Grande. Just this past year Tommy and a client taped a 228-pound fish they caught on live bait. That tarpon was the lead fish in a string that passed just out of range off my bow before meeting Tommy's skiff head-on.

To target one fish out of a school takes accuracy, timing, patience, and luck. It also takes a guide who has the eyes of a hawk. An angler fishing solo can't reasonably expect to quickly locate and cast to the largest fish in a string. Teamwork is the key.

For example, when casting to chaining fish, the guide positions the boat so the caster gets the best presentation possible. A guide looking for the single heaviest tarpon in a daisy chain stands a better chance of determining girth by eyeballing the individual fish on both sides of the chain when they are coming or going directly away. It's far more difficult to estimate the size of a fish when it is swimming broadside, a view that offers a clearer picture of the fish's length rather than girth, which is the most important factor in a tarpon's weight.

It takes patience for an anxious angler to await forthcoming casting instructions while the guide sizes things up. Once the guide locates the prime target, he never takes his eyes off of it. For instance, if the fish are swimming counterclockwise, once the target fish approaches the far right-hand side, the guide instructs his angler to begin making a cast to the left edge of the circle. (Remember, you

I've seen the leader slide down a tarpon's back and over its dorsal without spooking the fish.

must cast to the outside of the chain so the fly will be moving in the same direction as the tarpon when you impart action to it.) This anticipates the time it will take the target fish to make the balance of the half-circle trip while the fly is delivered and settles into place. Distance from and the diameter of the chain are important variables, but the concept remains the same. If the fly is early and lands in front of the fish ahead of the target fish, do not move it. Hopefully, the smaller fish will pass up the snack. Sometimes it works and

sometimes it doesn't, but it's a heart-stopping process all the same.

Chained-up fish are holding in one area. Picking the heaviest fish in an approaching string is a bit more difficult. If they are coming toward the skiff, the heavy fish is easier to spot, but timing is challenging. You can only scan the string quickly before making the cast. Barring a wide gap in the string that separates the target fish from the others, you most always cast in front of the lead fish. If the guide spots a "weight" fish farther back in the

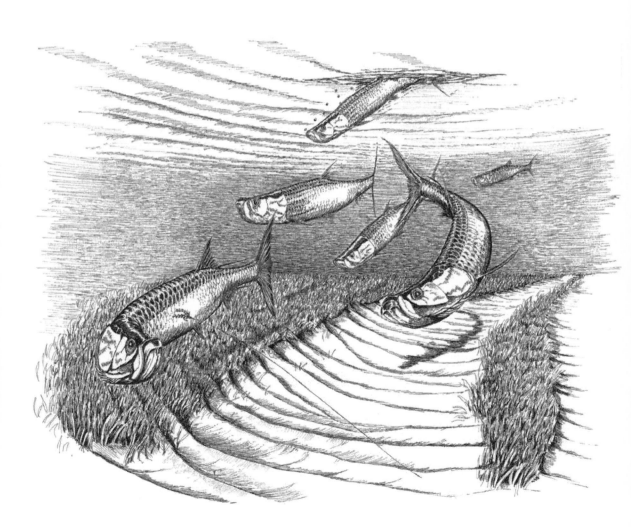

pack, he will instruct you how to react and you should respond accordingly.

Once you cast to the lead fish, you should not move the fly or line until the guide says so. You are waiting for the smaller fish to pass and the largest fish to come within range. As long as the fly or line aren't moving, fish often pay no attention to it. I've watched unwanted fish slow down to investigate a dead fly only to pass it by and swim on. I've also seen my leader slide down a tarpon's back and over its dorsal as it passes under without spooking the fish. However, all of your best efforts can go up in smoke by something as simple as the tail wash of a passing fish bringing your fly to life, despite your best efforts to keep it still.

The "A" Position

Most posting-up spots have an "A" position. In theory, this location gives the angler the best of all worlds for approaching fish. It normally offers the first fly presentation to the most incoming fish.

No matter where you go—the Keys, Boca Grande, and every other tarpon fishery I can think of—the "A" position is acquired on a first-come, first-served basis. Folks have slept on their boats to assure their position in a run.

As a rule, every position behind the "A" spot is less desirable because the anglers are typically casting at worked-over fish. The angler fortunate enough to be at the top spot carries a responsibility to the other anglers in line. For example, taking repeated casts at a string of fish is out of line and unnecessary. Odds are it won't prove productive and buggers up the fish even more for anglers down the line. Also, avoid taking low-percentage casts at fish traveling at more than 90 degrees to the boat; they are not really your fish in this situation. The skiff behind may be in a better position to feed these fish. Let them go. By the way, more times than not, once the tide drops down or comes up, the "B" spot often becomes the "A" spot, and the previous "A" spot is no longer a spot at all. What comes around goes around!

Hook-Sets

You watch in disbelief as a 120-pound tarpon stalks your fly. Its huge mouth opens, surrounding the tiny offering, and then your brain sends a 200-mile-per-hour message to your hands saying, "Do something stupid." In an instant, the tip of the fly rod shoots straight up toward the sky, and the fish comes unbuttoned after the first jump. Why? The hook point can't penetrate the tarpon's bony mouth with only the small amount of force generated by the rod's whippy tip.

Despite the tarpon's bony mouth, a properly sharpened hook will find a secure home with regularity if you react correctly during the strike, which takes some practice. I spent my first ten years fishing for tarpon in dirty water. As a result, I was rarely able to watch tarpon approach and devour a fly. I had to work on what I felt versus what I could see. Since I could not see the fish approaching the fly, I did not react to the strike until the fly line came tight. This is important. No matter what you see, don't react in any way until you feel the fish come tight. Don't bring the line tight with your rod tip. Let the fish do it for you.

Almost without fail, a tarpon will make a quick

turn left or right after engulfing a fly. It's really kind of amusing to watch. The tarpon eats and veers off like he just got away with doing something improper. This turn is one key to a good hook-set. Once in a blue moon, a tarpon will continue swimming toward you after eating. This makes it more difficult to get a good hook-set and forces you to attempt a hook-set before feeling anything. Lefty shared a great tip with me recently for hooking a fish that fails to turn. Simply stomp on the deck of the skiff and the fish will spook and turn.

The sudden change in direction does several things that work in your favor. First, the turn brings the fly line tight. This is what I was feeling, not seeing, all those years in the dark water of Mosquito Lagoon. The tarpon is tightening the line, not you. Second, turning brings the fly over to a corner of the fish's mouth. The direction of the turn dictates which corner. For example, a left turn draws the hook point to the right side of the mouth. Make a mental picture of which direction the fished turned. It will be useful during the fighting phase. I don't know why, but I can recall each direction a particular fish turned long into the fight. It's like my brain takes a snapshot. Of course, this is coming from the same guy that posted up on a run recently, only to discover I had left my fly rods back at the dock, lying across my fish cleaning table!

A well-sharpened hook should find a crevice or fold in the corner of the mouth to hang on, but now you must drive the point home. First, don't attempt to drive the point home on your own. The fish will help you, if you let it. Once the fish comes tight, bring the rod back and slightly to one side while holding the fly line securely in your left hand (if you are right-handed). All you want to do with your right hand is to create a small, forgiving angle from the rod to the fish. Pointing the rod directly at the fish will break the class tippet. Conversely, swinging the rod too far to the side won't work. The tip of the rod cannot set the hook! Twenty degrees or so uses the entire length of the rod, applying maximum pressure to the hook point, yet offers enough forgiveness to avoid breaking your leader. Now, hold that position while gripping the fly line in your left hand and pull back slightly. This strip-set sinks the hook point once it's found a place to call home. The amount

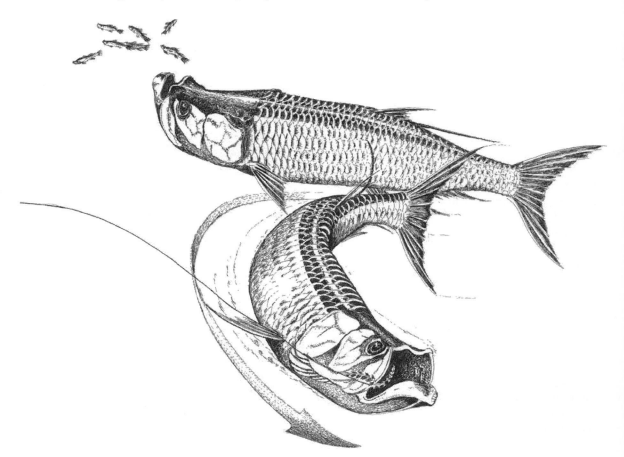

Once the tarpon eats the fly, it usually turns, which brings the hook into one corner of the fish's mouth and tightens the line.

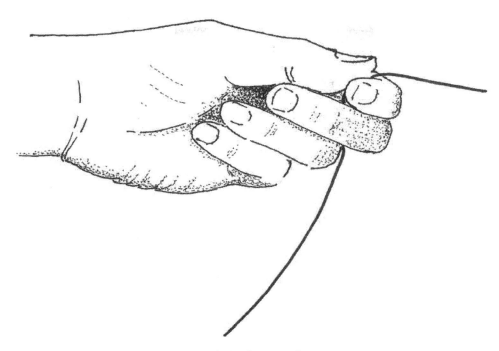

Weave the line in between your fingers to give you a good grip when you strip-set.

of pressure and length of time you set depends on the breaking strength of your leader and the initial surge of the fish. I cast, strip, and fight fish with the fly line woven between my fingers, which provides a nonslip grip on the line that I can release instantly (See "Fighting Fish," page 122).

Some anglers advocate taking a step backward during the hook-set, but I prefer shifting my weight to my back foot (my right foot). I do this by sliding my hips back. If I need to back off a little, I reverse this move. I think about the hook point penetrating the fish's mouth as I am setting the hook and can feel when I have done a good job driving the hook home.

The closer the fish is to the skiff when she eats, the better the hook penetration because there is less line stretch and more pressure applied directly to the hook point. For this reason, the potential for exceeding the class tippet's breaking strength is greater when the action is close to the boat.

If the fish surges or jumps before I feel I set the hook properly, I strike one to three times, using my left hand and full length of the rod. These are snappy, short, 6- to 8-inch strikes, and the action is like pulling on a rope during a tug of war. The entire slightly bent rod just slides backward, while the left hand grasps the line securely and pulls in unison with the rod hand. I often see anglers do this to extreme. Their rod waves wildly, and their left hand goes out to full extension as if they were trying to dislodge the fly from a mangrove limb.

CHAPTER THIRTEEN

Fighting Fish

The most difficult battle you'll ever encounter is when your adversary has more to lose than you—in fishing and in life. While you are fighting the tarpon for fun, she is fighting for her life. She has no clue your intent is to release her when it's over. Chances are she is much faster and agile in the water than you will ever be on dry land. She is also in better shape than you—even if you can bench 300 pounds. She is in her element and could care less about how big the seas are or how dehydrated you get. I've watched some pretty tough folks fold under the physical stress of doing battle with tarpon.

No two tarpon fight exactly the same. This is one of the things I love most about them. Size, sea conditions, water depth, and temperature all play a part in the duration and intensity of the fight, but each fish's individuality is the biggest difference between fish. Like track-and-field athletes, some specialize in the high jump, while others prefer the broad jump. Others are sprinters, covering water at a blistering speed, while some prefer marathons, displaying unparalleled endurance. Then there are the fish that view the skiff's hull as their own per-

sonal obstacle course, darting under the boat at every opportunity. Like a gift, you don't have a clue about what is inside until you take off the wrapper. Once things settle down a bit and you begin applying pressure on one another, you will learn a lot about the type of fish that you have hooked.

Over time, you begin to categorize various fish: jumpers, runners, bottom-huggers, boat-huggers, fighters, and quitters. You'll get surprised now and then, but for the most part tarpon are pretty much like folks—when they get in trouble, their individual personalities show through.

No two veteran tarpon fighters will make the same moves at the same time during a fight. Just as in boxing, each will have his own style and technique. No doubt some folks place greater importance on some things and less on others I cover in this chapter. Even though seasoned tarpon fighters might disagree on various tactics, they all have the goal to catch and release the tarpon as quickly and efficiently as possible. If you react to the tarpon's movements, you will fight the fish too long. You need to take the initiative as soon as possible and never relinquish that position until the fish is in hand. Too many tarpon battles go on far too long due to poor fighting skills and bad boat handling.

Unlike casting, you cannot learn to fight fish in your backyard. Sinking a hook in a fence post won't tell you much about the inside of a tarpon's mouth. Reading about fish fighting will only get you so far. Watching it done by professionals like Stu Apte, Flip Pallot, and Lefty Kreh is far more beneficial. Doing it yourself? Well, that's unforgettable.

The Miracle Minute

You're really not charged with doing much in the seconds following a good hookup. It's more about not doing certain things, such as not standing on your fly line. Look down at your feet. When, James Taylor sings in "Country Road," "I guess my feet know where they want me to go," he wasn't thinking about fly fishing off the front deck of a tarpon skiff. Your feet don't know. They will go right on top of the coiled fly line on your deck if you let them.

After the solid hookup, separate your two hands by aiming the rod tip forward and far out toward the fleeing fish. Your left hand should be stretched outward slightly and down from your side so you keep your hands a safe distance apart. I will explain why in a minute. The remaining fly line coiled on the deck is going to follow that tarpon. I promise, she will take that and then some, and she will do it in a hurry. Don't let go of the fly line. Some folks like to let the line pass through a circle formed with their thumb and pointer finger, but I prefer to let it slide in the crevices of the second joint of my fingers. Either way, guide that last bit of loose line all the way to the reel.

Keeping the rod hand and line hand separated is essential until the last inch of fly line is cleared

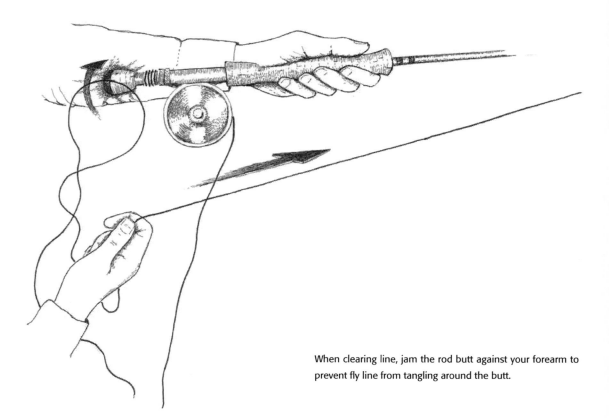

When clearing line, jam the rod butt against your forearm to prevent fly line from tangling around the butt.

from the deck and the fish is on the reel. In all the confusion and excitement, it's easy for the loose fly line to cross over or around the rod butt. If this occurs, you will probably break off the fish. To ensure the line doesn't snag on your rod butt, force it against your forearm while your rod is extended toward the fish.

No matter how well you master this process, once in a while things are still going to get screwed up. It happens to everyone. Just when you think you've got it figured out, you're going to look down and a wad of fly line the size of a plate of spaghetti will be lifting off the deck. Stuff happens. If it's just a loop or two, you might be able to use a trick that Lefty Kreh taught me. Simply flip your

fly rod upside down. The reel and the rod guides should be facing up instead of down. The tangle is more likely to slide through the snake guides of the bent rod in this position because the knot is running along the fly rod blank instead of popping over the guide's wire.

This time belongs to the tarpon. Your job is to stay hooked up until she has finished her initial jumps and runs and begins to settle down.

The Jumps

A jumping tarpon is a beautiful sight. Not only is it breathtaking to see the fish airborne, its head appearing to be attached to its body on a hinge, but

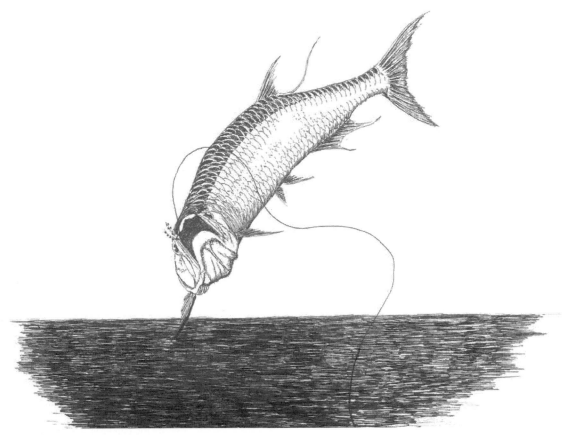

When a tarpon jumps, you must impart slack in the line.

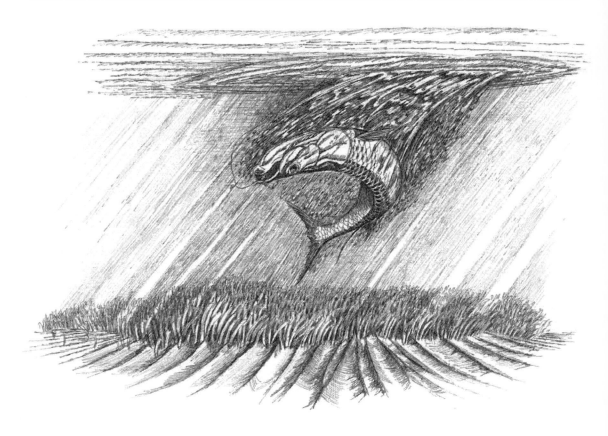

Once a fish lands back in the water after a jump, it pauses—perhaps because it is disoriented or it is getting back into an upright position. Take advantage of this pause to apply pressure.

each jump eats away at the tarpon's energy, which works in your favor. The trick is to get through each jump without losing the fish.

When a fish jumps, it is critical to impart slack in the line because a taut leader can be broken easily given the weight, speed, and power of a leaping tarpon. Things happen more quickly in the air than underwater. Head shakes, rattling gill plates, and the large body falling on a leader can easily break a 16-pound tippet. Perhaps due to their weight and size, large fish rarely clear the water. A tarpon over 160 pounds lunges forward, and if her head is above the water, you must give slack or she will break the class tippet.

You can add slack to the line with a number of different methods, but no matter which one you use, it's advantageous to be able to anticipate the jump. Watch for the portion of fly line closest to the fish to begin rising or when the fish surges suddenly. It takes speed and inertia for a 100-pound fish to clear the water. Your line and rod will telegraph the fish's movements.

Anglers are often told to "bow to the fish" when it jumps. Bowing forward while also extending the rod adds slack in the line. After the fish jumps, anglers pull their rod hand back to their body, cupping the bottom of the reel or handle with their other hand.

If I am standing on a raised casting platform, I bow. But when I am not, I add slack to the line by taking a short step toward the fish with my forward foot, leaving my rear foot planted. Since I am right-handed, I almost always step with my left foot. When the fish hits the water, I simply slide back into fighting position. Not only is this method faster, it helps me stay balanced on a pitching deck in rough seas.

After the jump, the fish hesitates briefly before making its next move. Perhaps it is disoriented or getting into positioning to start swimming again. Things don't happen as quickly underwater, even

for fish. Take advantage of this time and apply pressure, keeping the fish off balance, before the fish regains its composure.

Using Both Hands

I grew up using spinning reels, so I assumed that you reeled a fly reel with your nondominant hand. Lefty Kreh convinced me that I should reel with my dominant hand—it is both faster and gives you more endurance. That means if you are right-handed, you should reel with your right hand. Most folks, regardless of how tough they are, can't

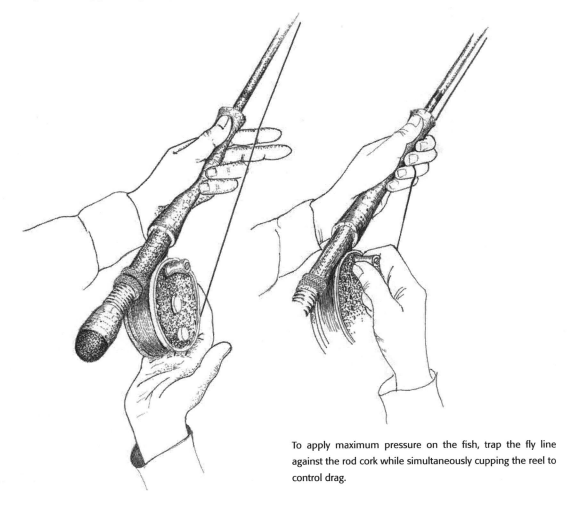

To apply maximum pressure on the fish, trap the fly line against the rod cork while simultaneously cupping the reel to control drag.

Fly-reel drags should be smooth and tightened only to prevent the spool from overrunning. MARK HATTER PHOTO

reel at a steady pace long enough to recapture the line necessary to regain control of the fish when reeling with their nondominant hand.

The rod hand can do a lot more for you than grip the cork handle. If you trap the fly line against the rod cork, you can stop the line with your hands, while simultaneously cupping the reel with your right hand to control the drag. It looks like it would be difficult to work the line into this position, but it's not. Your thumb will always be on top of the cork. When grasping the fly line, don't use all your fingers. Curl back two or three fingers out of the way, and grasp the line with what is left. I do this when casting and stripping as well so when I need a nonslip grip on the line, I can just close my fingers.

Both hands work in unison during a tarpon fight. First, I hold the fly line with one or two fin-

gers against the cork with my left hand. I can stop the line completely or feed it through my fingers with accurate pressure when I need to. I cup my right hand against the rails of the reel spool when I am not reeling so I can stop the spool completely or let it spin at any desired speed by simply adjusting the pressure. I change pressure depending on what I see and feel through the rod. With experience, it becomes a lot like driving a stick shift—you know what to do and when to do it by feel.

Though I think they should be smooth, I don't think fly-reel drags help you beat a fish, so I only tighten my drags enough to prevent the spool from overrunning. Using your hands to stop or control fly line enables you to apply maximum pressure on a fish. Applying pressure is not as hard as determining the *maximum* pressure the class tippet can endure. Since the breaking strength of 12-pound is less than 20-pound, maximum pressure will vary between the two. The amount of fly line that's off the reel will also impact the amount of pressure that can be applied because of the stretch in both your fly line and leader.

Balancing Act

With an afternoon sea breeze and a rocking boat, balance becomes critical. When I fight a fish, I am always searching for balance. If your legs are not in good shape, you are in a lot of trouble, because your legs help you stay stable under the shifting conditions. A lot of anglers that come fishing without their sea legs (which is understandable because they've been in Cincinnati, Ohio) are just whipped by 3 o'clock. Fighting a tarpon is physically demanding, so you should prepare for the encounter with strengthening exercises.

Pulling Anchor

Fighting a large fish while maneuvering a skiff can be challenging. Just getting rid of an anchor line quickly so that you can chase a tarpon can be difficult. I came up with a system for this a few years ago. I use a Wichard snap shackle to fasten my anchor line to the bow of the skiff and when I want to free my anchor, I yank a length of line attached to the shackle's pull pin. I retrieve my anchor (there is a float attached to the anchor line) when the fight is done, or simply rehook the shackle and resume fishing.

Taking Chase

Unless you dead-boat the fish, you have to take chase following the fish's initial run. I use an 82-pound-thrust bow-mounted trolling motor; however, in rough seas with giant fish, I sometimes need the outboard. Because you need to retrieve all the backing and fly line from the fish's surges, you should be reeling with your dominate hand. Reeling quickly for long periods can be exhausting. Don't pump the fly rod while retrieving line. This is not effective due to the amount of line that's out.

Your primary task is to stay up with the forward movement of the boat as you retrieve fly line. If you can't reel fast enough, slow the skiff down to prevent slack from forming, which can tangle around the rod tip as you reel. If this occurs the tangle will be 9 feet away. It might as well be a mile, and it will cost you a fish. Should you overrun the fish and slack gets in the line, lower the rod tip just under the water to either side of the bow and keep reeling. The drag of the water will minimize the rod's movements and loop the excess line back and away from the rod tip.

Once you have the fly line back on the reel, you cannot rest. When you rest so does the tarpon. You will pay dearly for letting a tarpon regain her strength during any stage of a fight.

What's the Rush?

Before discussing *how* to apply maximum pressure on a tarpon, I should discuss *why* you should. After all, what's the big rush?

The longer you fight a tarpon, the more you increase the odds of bad things happening. Hammerhead or bull sharks often attack struggling fish tethered to someone's line or lactic acid build-up or warm water stresses and eventually kills fish. Through the course of a long fish, the tarpon's sandpaperlike mouth grinds away at your bite leader and the entire tippet stretches under the pressure and weakens. Don't back off the pressure. Even if the fish doesn't die or get off from all of the above hazards, tarpon are good swimmers. If you don't stop the fish, you are likely to be heading for Mexico. Have a nice trip, and don't drink the water.

Keeping up the Pressure

Remember, you cannot set the hook securely in a tarpon's mouth by high-sticking the rod, because the whippy rod tip doesn't have the power to drive the hook point home. The same theory applies when fighting tarpon. Many anglers believe they are applying maximum pressure with their fly rods, but they aren't. Though an arching rod looks impressive, you apply more pressure with less of a bend. To apply maximum pressure to a tarpon, point the rod more toward the fish.

Flip Pallot has had a lot to do with the design of some of the great fighting rods over the years. The one-piece, 9-foot, 12-weight Cross Current (Loomis) that I use exclusively today was designed

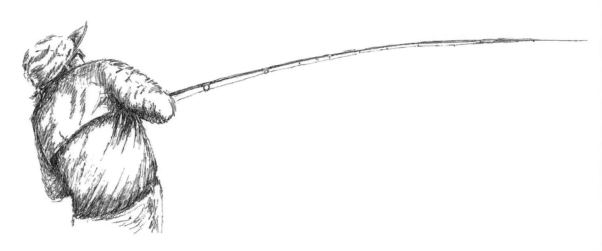

Correct angle for fighting a fish from the side.

Incorrect angle for fighting a fish from the side.

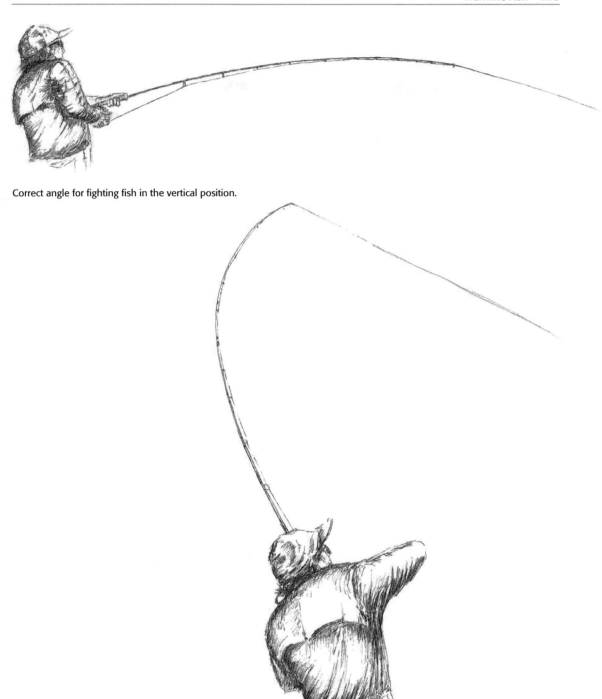

Correct angle for fighting fish in the vertical position.

Incorrect angle for fighting fish in the vertical position.

by Flip and legendary fly caster Steve Rajeff. A 9-foot fly rod allows casters to deliver the fly with stealth and grace, but that's only part of the game.

When it comes to fighting fish, only the butt section of the 9-foot lever is the most effective, and according to Flip, "the fighting portion of a rod is the first 25 inches outside the cork handle." The rest of the rod has pretty much done its job after it has delivered the fly. If you use the entire length of the rod throughout the fight, the longer lever actually favors the fish, and it is like bringing a sword to a knife fight. Turn your cumbersome sword into a knife by shortening the lever during the fight by reducing the angle of attack to about 10 to 20 degrees.

If you have ever been snagged on the bottom, you know that the easiest way to break your line is to point your rod at the fly and pull straight back. When fighting a tarpon, you want to try to pull almost straight back, but maintain just a slight bend in the rod, which is critical to protect your tippets.

Boat Work

Boat position relative to the fish is critical to beating a tarpon in a reasonable period of time. The perfect position of the boat is almost always directly behind the tarpon. This can change when the fish is close and tired. The girth of a large tarpon is massive. Is this really something you want to try and drag sideways in the water? Flip Pallot uses the analogy of pulling a large serving platter through the water: "Which way would be the most effective way of swimming it . . . broadside or on edge?" An osprey carries a fish through the air headfirst, not broadside.

Staying directly behind a tarpon allows you to pull back on the fish. Try to use the weight of the skiff to help apply pressure on the fish. The best situation is to have the boat downwind from the fish and thus pushing you away. While this would be a walk in the park if tarpon swam straight, they do not. When the fish angles, say to the left, the angler must react one way and the boat handler

When fighting a fish, remember that an osprey does not carry its prey broadside.

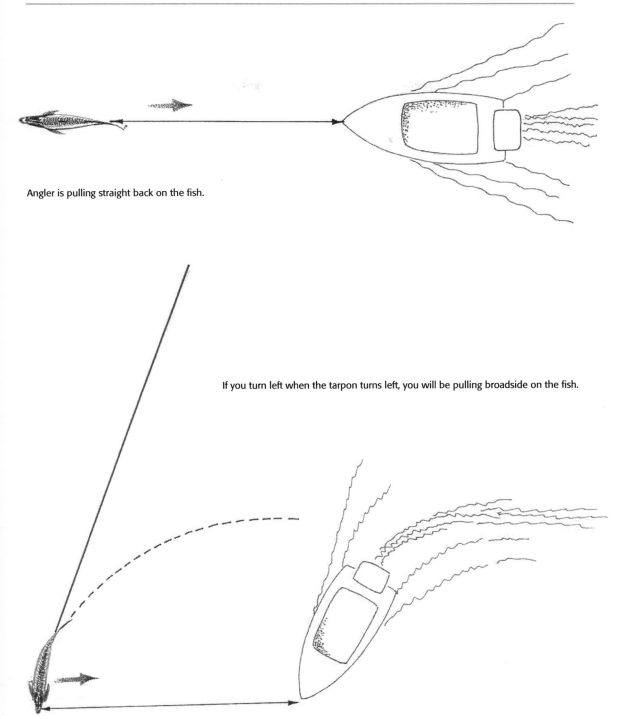

Angler is pulling straight back on the fish.

If you turn left when the tarpon turns left, you will be pulling broadside on the fish.

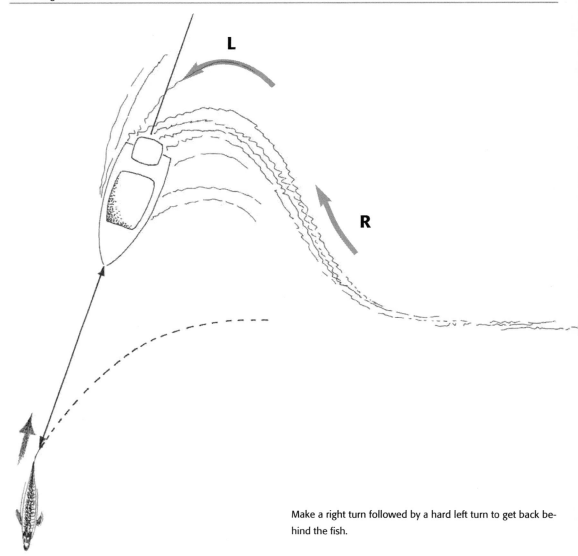

Make a right turn followed by a hard left turn to get back behind the fish.

another. The angler should pull the rod in the opposite direction the fish turned.

When the fish turns left, you need to get the skiff back into position. Draw an imaginary rigid straight line down the back of the fish and three boat lengths back (which should be your following distance). When the fish turned left, the imaginary line swung to the right of the skiff. The boat handler's job is to get the angler back on that straight line behind the fish using the shortest route. The quickest and most efficient way to do this is with a right turn. Once the bow of the skiff meets the imaginary line, make a hard left turn. Boat handling during a hard fight becomes an art form in itself.

You'll lose and regain line many times on a big fish. As the fight continues, you will be able to work within two boat lengths of the fish. During the fight, the fish will swim close to the surface. She probably needs to gulp air. Some folks suggest pulling her head down to stop her from getting air, but I've found that if a big tarpon wants air, she's going to take it. You won't be able to stop her. Not on 16-pound, and not with a crane.

The End Game

When the fight is nearing its end, the fish's tail kicks will slow when she begins to tire. She will also be swimming near the surface. Is the butt section of your fly line under her belly or over her back? It should be running down her back. Remember, she's hooked in the right corner and she's swimming straight away. The line should remain low, crossing over her back and exiting on the left side of the tail. Pull firm, steady, and low to the left trapping the line with your rod hand and cupping the reel to a stop with the other. Anticipate a reaction, because she's not going to like this. Your job is doing stuff she doesn't like. This down-and-dirty maneuver not only applies pressure directly back, but it twists her body over and to the left. You are using the angle created by the hook position to put her and keep her off balance. The trick is to maintain your balance and keep the tarpon from gaining hers. For the most part, the opponent who does this most effectively will be the one who is victorious.

Pulling back and twisting the fish is a down-and-dirty maneuver to keep the fish off balance.

An effective way to keep a tarpon off balance while chipping away at her energy reserves is to apply low side pressure in the opposite direction the tarpon turns. In the later rounds of battle, when she goes left, you should pull low and to the right. When she swings right, you should pull low and to the left.

Pulling in the opposite direction a tarpon turns is a good rule of thumb, but like most rules, there are exceptions. At times, pulling the face of a tarpon in the same direction she is turning can be the most effective move. Think of this like playing a game of chess. The right move might mean giving up a little to gain a lot. You might want to get into position or set the fish up for a specific maneuver such as positioning a tarpon for landing, rolling the fish over, recapturing line to eliminate stretch, or allowing the fight to move to shallower water or even upwind of the skiff. Additionally, turning a fish in the direction she is moving might be the quickest route to get the skiff directly behind the fish. This is often the case when fighting tarpon without a boat handler. These are calculated and orchestrated moves to help you gain and maintain the upper hand during a fight. In the absence of these things, pull the opposite direction the fish is turning.

When the tarpon begins wobbling when broadside to waves and working hard to remain upright she is getting tired. She also will ride near the surface, gulping air more frequently than before. The upper portion of her tail will protrude above the water, cutting her forward movement in half due to the loss of traction. Though the fish will not jump, she can still lunge forward, so be prepared.

Just because she's tired, don't think she's beat. This is when most fish are lost. Your leader is likely stretched and tired, and so are you. You also don't have the luxury of the fly line stretch to soften any of the fish's movements. Combat with a tarpon close to the boat takes quick and precise reactions. The margin for error increases as the distance between the angler and the fish reduces. If she turns in toward the skiff, stay nimble and move on the gunnels. Should she swim under the hull, strip additional line from the reel to buy time and move smoothly on around the bow or stern. Try to visually measure her strength. If you fight her too long, she may not revive. On the other hand, a green fish at the side of the boat can be more than you can, or wish to, handle.

Rolling the Fish

At the end of a fight, when there is one boat length or less between you and the fish, you can roll it over to make the landing process much calmer. It won't always work, but when it does it's a home run.

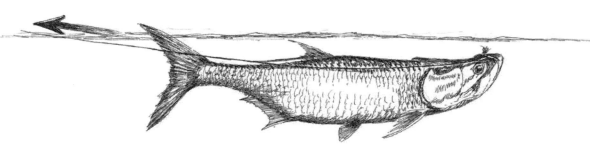

With the fish aimed directly away from you, carefully work the butt section and leader around a pectoral fin so it is running along the fish's belly.

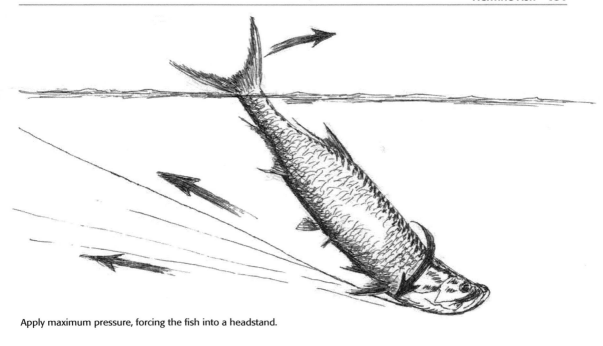

Apply maximum pressure, forcing the fish into a headstand.

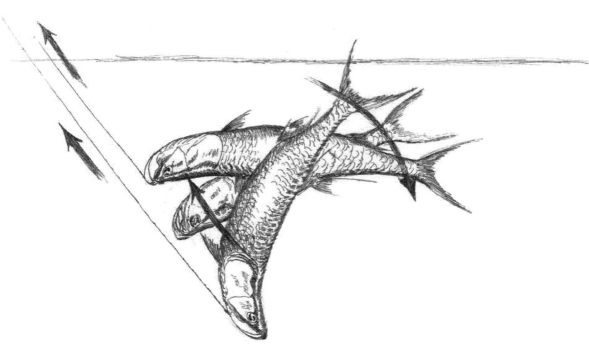

Lift up and back on the rod, so that she rolls upside down.

The fish must be aimed directly away and right on the surface. Once you carefully work the butt section and leader around a pectoral fin so it is running along the fish's belly, the person handling the boat should stop the forward progress of the skiff. Hold the line and cup the reel while lowering the rod tip below its body. Now gradually apply maximum pressure straight back, keeping the rod low. In essence you are attempting to use the fish's forward motion and your strength to force it into a headstand. When done correctly, the tarpon's tail will rise above the surface.

Once she is in this vulnerable position with her propeller out of the water, you must work quickly. Increase the angle between you and her head by lifting up and back on the rod. Step back if necessary. Your objective is to keep her coming toward you but in an inverted position. If she rolls over to an upright position, set the boat up for another attempt. Once upside down, the tarpon is finished. Most fish don't do well upside down. They often go into a trancelike state; for instance, snook, redfish, and bonefish lie motionless when inverted and this is a good thing to do when removing a hook. A recent conversation with Michael Larkin of Bonefish and Tarpon Unlimited may shed some light on the reason tarpon react this way when rolled over. In the absence of any real data, Larkin theorized the key may be found in the fact that tarpon use otoliths located in their ear bones to orient themselves. Larkin explains, "Think of otoliths as a dinner plate surrounded by nerves. The fish knows she is upright when the otoliths rest on the nerves at the bottom or base of the canal. When inverted, they rest on the nerves at the top of the canal." He expects this might have some physiological effect on the balance and orientation of tarpon, but this isn't proven to date.

Mind Games

There's more to fish fighting than the physical techniques I've discussed thus far. Mental gym-nastics also can come into play and are magnified with the size of the fish and the importance of the catch. When the stakes get high, most anglers become overly cautious, but that is the wrong approach.

I will never forget the monster tarpon I hooked on the beach in Boca Grande. To my dying day, I will believe she hit 220. She was hooked in the button, right smack dab in the center of the upper jaw—which, in my experience, is a bad, if not the worst, place in the mouth to hook a big fish. This is because it's very difficult to keep a big fish off balance unless she is hooked in one corner of the mouth. Chris Brouillette drove the boat while I tried to gain control of her. The huge fish swam steadily north up the beach, through Gasparilla Pass, and neared the old railroad trestle.

At this point, companions dropped longtime friend Charlie Madden off in my skiff. As we approached the trestle, Charlie warned, "If she swims under the railroad bridge, it's over." Support timbers blocked each of the 10-foot openings. They start above the water line, but angle down deep below the surface. A skiff can not cross under, but a tarpon can. She slipped under the railroad trestle and through the barricaded opening two boat lengths ahead of us.

There was only one option if I hoped to catch her. I jumped headfirst from the bow of the skiff. Had the tide been going out, I'd never have tried it. I thrust my fly rod straight ahead with one hand and protected my head with the other. To my utter amazement, I didn't touch a thing as I was swept under the surface by the current. By the time I bobbed up, I had cleared the span and was still hooked up. I glanced back to see Chris and Charlie kneeling on my front deck peering at me from the opposite side of the low railroad bridge. I am quite sure neither of them ever expected to see me again.

They hurried to an opening in the bridge some 300 yards away, sped around, and picked me up—literally—I was beat. I gasped for air as they hoisted me aboard. "Don't touch my rod," I said. IGFA rules dictate that only the angler can touch the rod involved in the fight for a record fish.

An hour later, I had a chance to take the tarpon, but I blew it. It's the only fish I've ever really brooded over losing. She crossed a shallow mud flat several miles inland from the trestle. Her tail kicks were slow and labored. She was partially on her side as she fought to clear the flat. I could have caught her right then and there. Charlie urged, "You can stop her now!" In retrospect I know now that was sound advice, but at the time I reasoned she might beach herself higher in the shallow mud. Tired fish in hot water make mistakes. So do anglers! At this stage of the fight, it was a contest to see who would make the first dumb mistake, and I won.

The huge fish eventually struggled across the flat and settled in a deep sand hole. She arched her back and spread her pectoral fins flat against the powdery white bottom. I pulled as hard as I dared with the stretched-out 16-pound-test leader, but it wasn't enough. As darkness settled in, we were stuck in a Mexican standoff no more than 10 feet apart. Eventually, she won. Every moment she stood her ground in the sand hole she recaptured her strength. That magnificent fish came out of that hole lunging back across the mud flat, and broke me off in deeper water. It was a long, dark ride home.

But, I learned something from that experience. On May 15, 2008, Tommy Locke and I were in Homosassa teamed up and trying to recapture over a hundred yards of backing as the huge fish steamed north. Out of courtesy for nearby anglers, we attempted to take chase with the trolling motor, but we were still losing considerable ground. Outside the ten-boat fleet, we finally started the outboard. She never jumped. I got a better look at her girth than Tommy when she ate but all I could swear to was she was big.

It took about twenty minutes from the time we hooked up before I wound my first wraps of fly line on the spool and started applying pressure. It wasn't until she was three boat lengths out she lifted her massive head above the water and Tommy verified, "We've got to get a tape on her." It was turning into a textbook fight with Tommy maneuvering the skiff directly behind and downwind from the fish. She was hooked midway from the left corner of her jaw to the button in the center.

I had a decision to make. I recall thinking about the fish that I swam for, and the mistakes I'd made. I told Tommy, "I'm going to fight her to win!"

Her tail kicks were slowing down, and she began wobbling in the waves brought about by a steady sea breeze. I began increasing pressure low and to the left and was able to stop her forward progress. Soon I was able to back her up, but each time I did, she circled back to the left and dropped down under the hull of the skiff about midship. I took enough slack from the reel to clear the bow, and Tommy repositioned the skiff for another attempt to bring her in.

After each attempt to bring her in, she circled to the left on our port side and ducked under the hull. After five or six attempts, I recall stepping farther to the stern and started applying pressure earlier than before, just as she emerged from under the starboard side, to bring about a tighter circle. Tommy was crouched on the port-side deck with outstretched gloved hands, when she angled under the hull. Tommy blocked my view of the fish. He gave sharp instructions, "Pull up and out. Now!" What I couldn't see was that the fish had hesitated just under the skiff and was now facing the bow. His instructions were on the mark. The giant fish slid out from under the shadow of the hull, and Tommy managed to slide one hand over her bottom jaw. His other hand followed abruptly, and his thumbs fought to find a hold underneath. I recall seeing his left foot wedged up and under the deck of the skiff to avoid being hauled overboard.

I removed the fly and stored the rod and leader out of harm's way. The tape and calculator were already within reach, and we began measuring the fish. I multiplied the girth (42.5) times her length (82.5), and the calculator spit out the result: 186.27 pounds. She was released exactly one hour after I sank the hook in her jaw. The current record held by well-known angler Tom Evans was 190.5 pounds, weighed on certified scales. According to the formula, this fish was short of the mark and stood the same chance of losing weight on the scales as she did gaining a pound or two. We were proud of our victory.

Taking A Break

I know some anglers have used weights and pulleys and even fence posts to determine the breaking strength of certain leader materials. But the best way that I've found to determine how much pressure a leader can take is to intentionally break some fish off. I'm not suggesting you hook up to the first tarpon of your life and then break it off on purpose just to determine the breaking point of your leader. However, sometime down the road learning the maximum amount of pressure you can apply (with a bend in the rod, not pointed directly at the fish) might be more important than catching another tarpon or two. To benefit from this exercise, you must tie all your leaders to the same specifications using the same leader material.

When you intentionally break fish off, your challenge is to upload and store what you feel in your hands into your hard drive upstairs. My hunch is that you will be surprised to find that the actual breaking point on a well-tied leader is greater than you believed. This is not an exact science, but once you've grasped when a specific leader gives way, you can begin applying something just short of the actual breaking strength of your tippets. With this information, you will catch more fish in less time.

CHAPTER FOURTEEN

Safe Landings

If you do not have experience grabbing a giant tarpon, you might find yourself a bit intimidated as you measure the size and power of your opponent up close. You should be. Even though you have won a large part of the battle by bringing the fish to the boat, you should follow some simple rules to ensure the safety of the fish and the person grabbing it. Here are some tips to help you get a grip.

Make Sure the Fish is Tired

When you are fishing alone and want to land and revive the fish, it is essential that the fish is tired. Obviously, the objective in fighting any fish is to land it successfully, but that can't occur until the battle is over. Because there is always a sense of urgency to either release the fish or measure her for record or tournament purposes, somebody needs to make the call that the fish is tired enough to be landed. A green fish, one that is still too fresh to handle, can be dangerous, and a fish that is fought for too long can die from exhaustion and lactic-acid building up in her system.

In most cases, once you can stop the fish's forward progress, you are close to being able to land the fish, but do not assume that the fish is going to cooperate. Tarpon aren't fond of being manhandled.

Once I fought a huge fish to the boat and watched her jump square on Flip Pallot's back as he attempted to grab her. He wasn't injured, but he got the stuffing knocked out of him. Then there was the fish Lefty brought to the skiff with Pallot and me cheering on. She came to the gunnel too fast and too green. I couldn't hold her. Her bottom jaw slammed into the right side of my forehead. I managed to get a good grip on the next pass when Lefty asked, "Where's all the blood coming from?"

Catching and releasing a giant tarpon when you're alone is exciting. I've done it many times. The trick is in knowing when it's safe to set the rod down and grab the fish. I have always found my incentive in holding firmly to the jaw of the tarpon on the first go around is substantially enhanced by glancing over at my unattended fly rod. If you're alone don't fight a fish any longer than you would if someone else was on board. The idea that she should be beat down further because you are doing this without help isn't fair or considerate to the fish's health. It's not her fault nobody is with you.

Go to the Clean Side of the Boat

When nearing the final stages of the fight, guide the fish toward a smooth, unobstructed portion of the deck. The push pole is generally mounted on the skiff's starboard side. Stay clear of the pole and the holders.

Grab, Don't Gaff

Many photos show anglers lifting tarpon out of the water with a lip gaff for a picture. I elect not to use lip gaffs on tarpon because of the significant thrashing that takes place once a tarpon is gaffed through the lower jaw. The tarpon's head often bangs severely against the boat. The gaff often pulls out, and then you have to gaff it a second time.

Tarpon eat by sucking in their prey. The lower jaw drops and the huge gill plates flare, creating suction through the mouth. Gaff holes through

Guide Tommy Locke and angler work together to land the fish on the clean side of the boat. MARK HATTER PHOTO

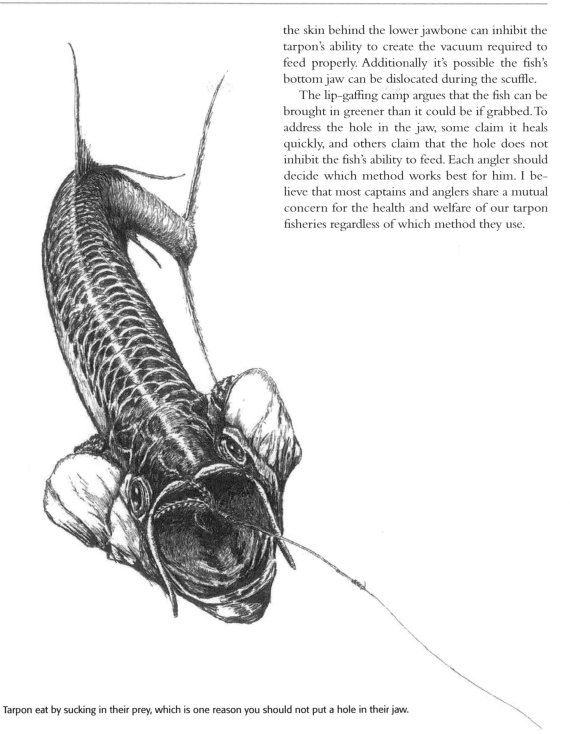

the skin behind the lower jawbone can inhibit the tarpon's ability to create the vacuum required to feed properly. Additionally it's possible the fish's bottom jaw can be dislocated during the scuffle.

The lip-gaffing camp argues that the fish can be brought in greener than it could be if grabbed. To address the hole in the jaw, some claim it heals quickly, and others claim that the hole does not inhibit the fish's ability to feed. Each angler should decide which method works best for him. I believe that most captains and anglers share a mutual concern for the health and welfare of our tarpon fisheries regardless of which method they use.

Tarpon eat by sucking in their prey, which is one reason you should not put a hole in their jaw.

Get Down

Lie flat with your chest on the deck and your knees on the floor. In some cases it may be necessary to lock your feet under the gunnels so the fish do not take you for a ride. I typically remove my hat and sunglasses. I'm planning on getting wet, and I don't want to be trying to focus through wet lenses or lose my hat.

Grasp the bite leader, not the class tippet, with one hand, and guide the fish's face into your other hand. It may take several attempts to get the angle right and the bottom jaw to open. It's not unusual for a fish to come to the boat backward because the angler is pulling her back. This is a difficult angle because you are reaching over the fish's back in an attempt to open her mouth and grab her lower jaw. I prefer grabbing the jaw with my right hand if

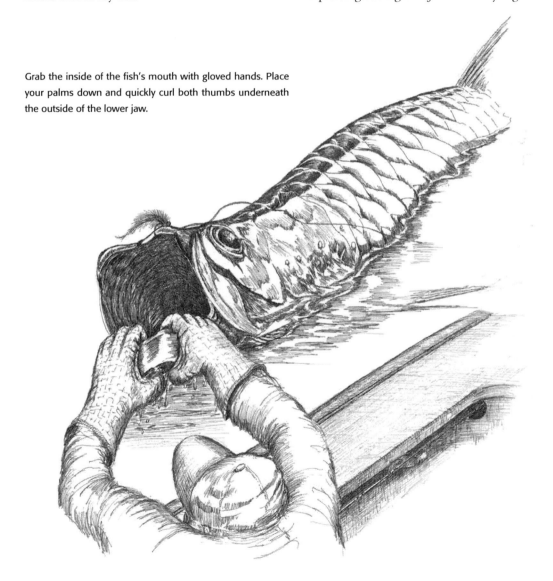

Grab the inside of the fish's mouth with gloved hands. Place your palms down and quickly curl both thumbs underneath the outside of the lower jaw.

possible. Because of that, I like to see the fish brought in horizontal to the skiff from my right to left. This dictates that the angler should be on the bow. It most certainly doesn't always work out that way, but that is what I consider a perfect angle.

Getting the fish's mouth to open can be a bit of a trick, though pressure on the bite leader along with a bit of prying with your fingers can help. Once you are grabbing the bite leader, instruct the angler to impart slack in the line. The last thing you want is the fly to launch out of the tarpon's mouth and end up stuck in you. Once you are grabbing the leader, there is no need for the angler to stay tight, but the angler should stay at the ready to resume the fight if the person grabbing the fish can't keep a firm grip.

Grabbing the Fish

The inside of a tarpon's mouth isn't a place for bare hands. Promar makes a pair of gloves that provide a good grip. I place my palm and thumb down. If you grab a big tarpon with your thumb inside the mouth, you have little or no protection for your face if the fish surges toward you. Additionally, if the fish arches down in this position, you can't compensate without lifting your entire body because your arms can't bend down beyond a horizontal angle to the deck in this position.

Grab the bottom jaw like you mean it with the palm down with one hand and the other just under the forward lower portion of the gill plate. Be cautious not to insert this hand too far into the gill opening, as gills are easily damaged. Quickly curl both thumbs underneath the outside of the lower jaw with your fingers over the top.

Don't Fight the Fish

Be prepared for some commotion. The fish will violently thrash its head and body. Hold on, but don't try to fight the tarpon. Go with the fish's movements using the flex in your arms. If possible,

Another view of the proper way to grab a fish.

do not let go. When the fish settles down, you may not be in the same spot on the deck as when you started. This is why you need to guide the fish to the unobstructed side of the skiff. You don't want a push pole holder wedged in your rib cage. You won't need to hunt around for pliers to remove the fly since you are wearing them on your belt or the angler will have gotten them ready for you.

The Photo Finish

Once the fish is quiet, move efficiently about the business of removing the fly, taking photographs, and taping the fish. Have the camera out and ready before grabbing the fish. It's a bad time for someone to be rummaging around in a tackle bag searching for more film. There must be a real sense of urgency in place when dealing with a tired fish. If the water temperature is high, time is even more critical.

When taking a picture, don't drag the fish out of the water by its lower jaw. This is not a handle for lifting fish. It's a hinged jaw held in place by muscle. Don't bring the fish inside the boat. I have

an old photo with me sitting on my deck with a 125-pounder stretched across my lap, and I cringe each time I look at it. Hang out over the side and take your picture. Using the skiff's rub rail as leverage to slide a huge fish up can easily break or damage its ribs.

Weighing In

It is now illegal in Florida to bring a tarpon on board a vessel without inserting a tarpon tag through its bottom jaw. Tarpon tags must be used before taking possession of a tarpon, which includes bringing one on board. Bringing a fish alongside the boat and holding it long enough to remove the hook does not constitute possession.

Should you wish to estimate the fish's weight, take accurate measurements of both its girth and

Take a picture of the fish by hanging out over the side of the boat. Never bring a fish inside the boat. After a quick photo session, revive the fish before releasing it. MARK HATTER PHOTO

length with a seamstress cloth-type tape. I keep the tape, camera, tarpon tag, and calculator in a watertight bag on the skiff. Measure the fish's girth slightly forward of its dorsal fin, where it's greatest. Measure length from the tip of the fish's nose to the fork of the tail. Square the girth, multiply this number by the length, and divide by 800 for a very close estimate. This is a two-person job. If you're alone, guess high.

Reviving the Fish

You should revive a spent tarpon before releasing it. While holding the fish, motor forward with your outboard or trolling motor to get water flowing through the mouth and across the gills. I hold the lower jaw down with one hand and grasp the upper lip with the other. This way I can create a large opening for more volume of water to pass through. The fish's first signs of recovery will be gentle tail kicks followed by head movement or its jaw might tighten on your grip. When you release the fish, make sure it stays upright.

During a fight, you should break a fish off if a shark tries to attack the tarpon. When you are handling the fish, keep a sharp eye out for marauding sharks. Shyness is not one of the characteristics of a giant hammerhead or bull. A tired fish just released is vulnerable. Once the fish is out of your grasp there is really little that can be done. Sometimes circling the shark or the tarpon with the skiff or racing the engine in neutral can help deter the attack.

Records

To kill a tarpon for record purposes, you must purchase and attach a tarpon tag to the fish. In Florida, the tag costs $50, and those purchased by professional guides are transferable to their clients. Very few tags are actually used. Records indicate that only 9 of the 344 tags issued in 2006 were reported as being used. Aside from world-record fish and those individuals wishing to have a skin mount, there is little reason to harvest tarpon. Fortunately, tarpon aren't good table fare.

There are many talented anglers who don't care about having their name in the record books. I respect them, and I have no doubt that the elusive 200-pounder has been landed on 16-pound on numerous occasions. For reasons known only to those anglers, the fish were released. I won't. She'll be deader than Grover Cleveland if I land her. I must confess I'm not bridled with sensitive feelings about killing a record tarpon. I certainly have the right to change course on this thinking; however, this is clearly one of those decisions best made in advance. Killing is serious business.

I keep a small zipper bag that includes a small camera, flexible tape, calculator, tarpon tag, and a tampon inside my tackle bag in the event I catch a record fish. I expect everything in the bag is understandable except the tampon. The object is to get the record fish to certified scales as soon as possible with as little weight loss as possible. There will be some, but it can be minimized by keeping everything that's already in the fish, inside. You stuff a towel in the fish's mouth and use a tampon for the other end. Both are removed at the time of weigh in.

An official IGFA application must be used to submit for a record fish. Photos are also required of the fish, rod and reel, angler, and certified scales. The fly, tippet, and butt section intact along with 1 inch of fly line must be submitted as well. The class tippet will be tested to make sure it falls within the required breaking strength for the line class for which the record is being submitted.

CHAPTER FIFTEEN

Reflections

Summer 1980, 4:30 AM. I balance a steaming cup of coffee in one hand, fidget with the radio dial with the other, and steer the Ford down the foggy black road with my knees. Billy was riding shotgun.

"Please son, don't spill your hot chocolate on the seat of my truck."

I couldn't see much through the windshield and less through the rearview mirror. I could only assume my skiff was still in tow. I saw it 5 miles back when we stopped at the convenience store. I loaded the rods and tackle boxes in the boat the night before.

That's when the hot chocolate jumped out of Billy's cup. It was inevitable. I turned on the interior light. "Yep. All over my damn seats."

Then, as if it happened yesterday, I recall exactly what I said next: "Why the hell don't you grow up and act like a man?"

His tearful reply has stayed with me for twenty-eight years: "Because daddy . . . I'm only six years old!"

. . .

Summer 2007, 4:30 AM. I scarcely hear the knock on the door. "Dad, can I go fishing with you this morning?" I was surprised to see Billy vertical at this hour. We had been together the night before on the island at an annual gathering of his buddies, and it had only been three hours when I saw him last. The Red Bucket Tournament had become a ritual by then. It's no tournament at all but rather twenty-five adults acting like kids who attack Boca Grande Island.

It wasn't always called the Red Bucket. A few years before, Billy and two of his buddies decided to leave all of their rods and tackle in their boat overnight. When they stumbled to the slip the following morning, everything was gone. So much for the good old days. A thousand dollars later, they were back in the game. There was a shortage of tackle boxes at the tackle store, so they stuffed everything in three red 5-gallon buckets.

Each trip I am invited, and each year I go. I am the old guy. I'm not all that concerned about getting older, but the idea of forgetting what it was like to be young scares me.

Billy and I pulled away from my dock about forty-five minutes behind schedule. Janie loves it when the kids stop in. She values fussing over them. You know, breakfast, coffee, pack some lunch and snacks. For most moms, 4:30 AM might be pushing the envelope. Not for her. Janie is in a league of her own.

The ride across the harbor was a little sloppy. Billy rode on the top seat with me. He pushed hard with his foot on the strut to lock himself firmly in place. He's had three back surgeries.

For the past week I had been working fish south of the harbor, but there was always something that kept it from going off. One day the wind blew out of the north. Tarpon hate a north wind. The next day it blew out of the south, but it never dropped below twenty. "Today looks good," I said, as we idled in and shut down. We could see slow rolling fish all moving south. I cranked up and made a wide circle to get ahead of them at the end of the bay where a bar running from east to west separates the bay from the open water of the sound. I used the trolling motor to move toward the far southeast corner of the basin and dropped anchor. It didn't take long for us to realize we needed to relocate the skiff another 30 feet back into a small dent in the edge of the bar. The fish were coming mostly in pairs or three-ships. No big strings. They slid in the dent and curled at a 45-degree angle to the skiff. "It doesn't get any

better than this," I said, as Billy slid his fly rod from the rack.

I love to watch Billy cast. We have much the same build and style, but he is left-handed. As he started to work the rod, I laughed to myself, *It's like watching my reflection.*

I didn't see the first fish eat, but I saw her turn after she had. I watched as she grey-hounded past the bow and took flight again toward the open water of the basin. I always get a better look at a fish when it's hooked to another angler's fly rod. She was a hundred pounds.

I went for the anchor line when Billy said, "Let me see if I can beat her without lifting the anchor."

I agreed. "Just remember that's 16-pound you're fishing."

"I know," he grunted back under the strain of the fish. "Let me grab her when she gets boatside."

He did—in fifteen minutes.

Over the next three hours, Billy jumped ten, fought seven, and caught five. We pulled anchor only on the last fish, a 140-pound bruiser that didn't have an ounce of quit in her. She met her match. Billy held her by the bottom jaw until she safely eased away.

The harbor was uncharacteristically calm on the way home, so Billy stretched out on the floor of the boat, the fight out of him. The light skiff took on a life of its own as it shimmied along, feeling

like a ride at the fair. As I drove to the other side, I kept stealing glances to watch him sleep.

• • •

I'll stack my daughter, Shannon, up with anybody who ever stepped on the bow of my skiff. Aside from the fact that she's an accomplished angler who throws a beautiful fly line, she's a spectacular person, wife, mother, daughter, and friend. Some folks can cast farther than her, but few can quickly and efficiently place the fly precisely where it needs to be when it really counts. She's jumped and caught more tarpon than most will in a lifetime.

In midsummer 2007, Shannon's left leg was in a cast due to a skiing injury that winter (a sport Floridians have no purpose engaging in). We pulled away, and soon we were posted on a beach run. She was propped up on her good leg in the

forward casting tower, cradling my new 12-weight and sparkling gold Tibor reel. I was in the stern with a second rod for backup.

Recent storms and strong tides had cut through a sandbar that jutted out from the desolate beach. The gap started against the shoreline and continued west about 75 feet or so. Beyond the cut, the sandbar jutted out for another 150 yards, the tip making a gradual curl to the north. On high tides, the bulk of the fish pushed from the south against the beach. On low tides, they would bypass the gap and follow the outer edge of the bar. We arrived on the first half of a falling tide. For the moment there were two " A" spots. That would change with lower water. The fish were making a good push. There were as many cutting through the gap as were turning outside.

We were anchored midway in the cut. Tommy Locke and a client I met years before were posted on the outside edge. The angler is a nice fellow who has spent his life living in New York City and has never owned a car. His annual trip to Florida includes tarpon fishing during the day and driving the wheels off the rental car each night.

As usual, Locke was leaning on his push pole, calling shots to his sport from the platform. I could see a good string of tarpon working our way tight to the beach 40 yards out. Before I could make the call, Shannon announced, "I got them, Dad!"

There's something empowering about being set up in exactly the right spot on an approaching string of tarpon. It's similar to sitting in a perfectly placed tree stand watching a buck of a lifetime slip into range.

The fish glided into position. Shannon had already released the fly from her left hand to begin her backcast, when I noticed a single fish slipping in from the opposite direction. We call these back-door renegades "crazy Ivans." I let my fly roll out ahead of the tarpon with a short backhanded cast.

She ate at the exact instant the lead fish of the approaching string from the south inhaled Shannon's offering. Both tarpon passed in midair, flying in opposite directions. It was an unforgettable sight. I broke mine off without hesitation, not wanting to cause more confusion than I already had. I quickly released the anchor line and took chase after Shannon's fish with the outboard. As it made its second jump, I put her at 130 pounds or so.

Shannon went through the initial moments of the fight like she really meant it, but the hard chop proved to be too much punishment on her knee. Any other time she would have beaten the fish, but she wisely concluded to break it off. I told her not to go down that mountain.

A large swell crossed the bar and crested over the bow, causing Shannon to fight for balance. When the rod and reel slipped from her grasp, the fly line was stretched like a bungee cord, and the rod, still securely connected to the tarpon, splashed down a boat length away. I was astounded by two things that were happening simultaneously. First, I

could see glittering flashes of sunlight bouncing off my shiny Tibor as it skipped like a flat river stone across the rough surface. Its last heading was due west when it finally ducked under. Second, a string of expletives that would make any pirate proud rolled like thunder out of my precious daughter's mouth. I reckon those apples do end up close to the tree. I couldn't stop laughing.

For reasons that denied common sense, I continued idling in the general direction of my fly rod's last sighting. I glanced at Tommy still balanced on his platform.

"Where's Shannon's 'poon?" he yelled.

"Cancun," I said, pointing west. "The fish is pulling the fly rod instead of the other way around." Tommy looked at me in disbelief.

Locke's skiff was still well to my port side when I saw him drag his push pole beneath the water like an oar. *No way,* I thought. He repeated the maneuver again, only this time I could make out the bright orange backing from my reel draped over the tip of the pole. I learned later Tommy never saw a thing. It was a wild shot in the dark. As he lifted the pole, the line began its descent. I had already spun my boat toward his, and I gave it some throttle.

The backing was still slightly above Tommy's grasp when my fly rod launched out of the Gulf of Mexico like a Polaris missile. In his younger days, Locke was a catcher in the minor leagues for the Braves. As far as I'm concerned, this was the best play he's ever made. "You can still catch," I laughed, as he snatched the fly rod from the sky.

As I idled past the stern of Tommy's skiff, he politely handed the outfit to Shannon, saying, "I think you might have dropped this. I believe there's still a good fish on the other end." We idled off, following an endless trail of bright orange backing, and once several wraps of fly line were on the spool, Shannon broke the fish off without further incident.

Index

Anchor
   pulling, 123
   selecting, 54–55
   strategies, 61
"A" position, the, 111
Apte, Stu, 1, 43, 118
Atlantic Ocean, 11, 16
Ault, Gerald, 7

Backhand cast, 97
Bass Pro Shops, 43
Biology and behavior
   future of the fishery, 16–17
   habitats, 11–14
   migration and spawning, 14–16
   overview of, 7–9, 11
Biology and Management of the World's Tarpon Fisheries (Ault), 7
Bishop, Bill (father of author), 4, 35, 45, 93
Bishop, Billy (son of author), 4, 6, 7, 52, 68, 143–145
Bishop, Janie, xv, 2, 6, 7, 144
Bishop, Shannon, 2, 7, 104, 144–148
Boats. *See* Skiffs, building/selecting; Skiffs, running
Boat slap, 61
Boca Grande, 7, 8, 68, 69, 74, 85, 86, 92, 109, 111
   fighting fish anecdote, 132–133
   fly selection, 33–36
   Red Bucket Tournament, 143
   running skiffs in, 57, 58
   skiff/gear selection, 49
   tarpon habitat described, 11–14
   tendon injury anecdote, 97–98
Boca Grande Pass, 17, 85
   fly selection, 33–34
   running skiffs in, 58, 65
   skiff/gear selection, 53
Body language
   busting tarpon, 83
   daisy-chaining tarpon, 81
   happy tarpon, 85–86

   laid-up tarpon, 69–72
   posting up on the beach, 72–74, 76
   rolling tarpon, 79–81, 130, 132
   screw-down tarpon, 81, 83
   tips from Locke, 81
Bonefish and Tarpon Unlimited (BTU), 17, 132
   PATs (pop-up archival transmitters), 15–16
Bonefish Research Project, University of Miami, 15
Brooks, Joe, 43
Broulliette, Chris, 92, 132–133
Brown, Randy, 38–39
Busting tarpon, 83
Butt section, 30–31

Captiva Pass, 7
Caribbean Sea, 11, 16
Casting
   backhand cast, 97
   curve cast, 94–96
   overview of, 93–94
   rod selection and, 93–94
   roll cast, 96–97
   tendon injury anecdote, 97–98
   tips from Kreh, 94–96
   underhand cast, 96
Catching fish
   See also Feeding fish; Fighting fish; Landing fish
   alert, staying, 87
   fly line management, 87–88
   optimism, 90–92
   pace, 92
   physical conditioning, 92
   preparation, 89
Charlotte Harbor, 12
Chassahowitzka River, 13
Chittum, Hal, 44, 49
Class tippet
   connecting to bite leader, 27–28, 30
   finishing, 30
   tying, 21–22, 26

Clouser Minnow, 36
Cockroach fly pattern, 35, 39–40
Connections. *See* Leaders and connections
Crystal River, 13
Curve cast, 94–96

Daisy-chaining tarpon, 81
Dewees, Bud, 45–46, 48
Dixon, Jay, 2
Domecq, Max, 11
Doparik, Al, 14

Enrico Puglisi (EP) baitfish pattern, 35–37
Englewood, 7, 45
Etiquette, 58–59, 64
Evans, Tom, 134
Evans, Tom, Jr., 14
Everglades, 11, 12

Fanny pack, inflatable SOS, 52–53
Feeding fish
    the "A" position, 111
    Locke and, 99, 109
    overview of, 99, 101
    practical advice, 101–104, 106–107, 109–111
Fighting fish
    balancing, 123
    boat position, 126, 128
    breaking off the fish, 134
    chasing, 123
    end game, 129–130
    jumps, 119–121
    mind games, 132–134
    miracle minute, 118–119
    overview of, 117–118
    pressure, keeping up the, 124, 126
    pulling anchor, 123
    rolling the fish, 130, 132
    using both hands, 121–123
Finding fish
    back country, slip hunting the, 69–72
    laid-up tarpon, 69–72
    overview of, 67–68
    posting up on the beach, 72–74, 76
    secret spots, 67, 77
    seeing the fish, 69, 76
Fishing Knots (Kreh), 20, 30
Flies
    conditioning and, 42
    connecting fly to bite leader, 26–27

as convenient snack, 41
    IGFA specifications, 36
    from the masters, 40–41
    overview of, 33–34
    patterns of, 35–40
    size, profile, and color of, 34–35
    standing out in a crowd, 42
    tips from Kreh, 40, 42
    tips from Madden, 38
    tips from Pallot, 40
Florida Fish and Wildlife Commission, 17
Florida Keys, 8, 27, 28, 30, 32, 44, 68, 85, 111
    fly selection, 33–36, 38–40
    tarpon habitat described, 12–14
Florida Keys Outfitters, 40
Florida Marine Research Institute, 17
Fly Fishing in Salt Water (Kreh), 45
Fly Fishing in Salt Waters (magazine), 6
Fly line management, 87–88
Fly line tamer, 54
Fulford, Pat, 6, 77
Future of the fishery, 16–17

Gaff
    kill, 55
    lip, 136–137
Gamakatsu SC 15 hook, 43
Gasparilla Pass, 132
Gear, skiff
    anchor system, 54–55
    fanny pack, inflatable SOS, 52–53
    fly line tamer, 54
    GPS, 52
    kill gaff, 55
    kill switches, 53–54
    miscellaneous, 55
    push pole, 55
    water (for drinking), 54
Gordon, Tom, 49
GPS, 52
Gulf of Mexico, 16, 104, 148
    running skiffs in, 65
    tarpon habitat described, 11, 14

Habitats, 11–14
Happy tarpon, 85–86
Hell's Bay Boatworks, 49
Henriques, Leo, 57
Hill, Kenny, 104
Holcomb, Keith, xiii

Holland, Jim, Jr., 14
Homosassa, 7, 8, 59, 69, 85, 109
    fighting fish anecdote, 133–134
    fly selection, 36, 39
    skiff/gear selection, 51, 52
    tarpon habitat described, 11–14
Homosassa River, 13
Hooks
    selecting, 40, 42–44
    tips from Kreh, 40
Hook-sets, 113–115
Hughes, Bob, 49

International Game Fish Association (IGFA)
        rules/specifications
    application for a record fish, 141
    fighting for a record fish, 133
    flies, 36
    leaders and connections, 19, 21, 22, 26, 27
Islamorada, 40

Jackson, Alan, 45
Johnson gold spoon, 42

Keating, Richard, 38–39
Keys, the. See Florida Keys
Kill gaff, 55
Kill switches, 53–54
Kirkpatrick, Steve, 14
Knots, 41
    Bimini, 2, 20, 22, 26–28, 32
    Homer Rhodes, 26
    Huffnagle, 22, 27–28, 30
    Kreh Nonslip Loop, 26
    Slim Beauty, 28, 30
    tips from Kreh, 2, 20, 26, 30
    tips from Locke, 26, 28, 32
Kreh, Lefty, 26, 34, 43, 45, 113, 118, 119, 121
    casting tips, 94–96
    Fishing Knot,, 20, 30
    Fly Fishing in Salt Water, 45
    fly tips, 40, 42
    hook tips, 40
    knot tips, 2, 20, 26, 30

Laid-up tarpon, 69–72
Landing fish
    photos, taking, 140
    records, rules for, 141
    reviving fish, 141

    step-by-step, 135–141
    weighing in, 140–141
Larkin, Michael, 132
Leaders and connections
    backing to fly line, 32
    building the leader, 20–22, 26–28, 30–31
    butt section, 30–31
    connecting class tippet to bite leader, 27–28, 30
    connecting fly to bite leader, 26–27
    finishing the class tippet, 30
    IGFA specifications, 19, 21, 22, 26, 27
    knots, 2, 20, 22, 26–28, 30–32
    overview of, 19–20
    storing leaders, 31–32
    tying the class tippet, 21–22, 26
LeFiles fish camp, 1, 6, 45–46
Lefty's Deceiver, 36, 40
Lip gaff, 136–137
Locke, Tommy, 22, 39, 145–148
    body language tips, 81
    feeding the fish, 99, 109
    fighting fish anecdote, 133–134
    knot tips, 26, 28, 32
    as source of local information, 57
    tendon injury anecdote, 97–98
"Longest Day and Night, The" (Pallot), 6

Madden, Charlie, 91
    emergency repairs anecdote, 65
    fighting fish anecdote, 132–133
    fly tips, 38
    as source of local information, 57
Megalops atlanticus, 7
Migration and spawning, 14–16
Mims, 1
Moret, Sandy, 40, 41
Mosquito Lagoon, 1–2, 4–6, 14, 68, 69, 96, 113
    fly selection, 42
    secret spot in, 77
    skiff/gear selection, 45, 49
Mouse fly pattern, 35, 37–39
Mustad 34007 SS hook, 40, 42–44
Myakka River, 12

Oak Hill, 1
Olson, David, 39

Pallot, Flip, 1, 2, 4–6, 43, 44, 118, 135
    fly tips, 40
    "Longest Day and Night, The," 6

rod design, 124, 126
  skiff/gear selection, 49
  skiff-handling tips, 64
Pallot, Mrs. Flip, 2, 4
Pate, Billy, 14
Peace River, 12
Peterson, Scott, 49
Photos, taking, 140
Pine Island Sound, 97–98
Posting up on the beach, 72–74, 76
Push pole, 55

Rajeff, Steve, 126
Record fish, 1, 11, 14
  IGFA official application, 141
  IGFA rules for fighting, 133
Red Bucket Tournament, 143
Reviving fish, 141
Richards, Ronnie, 51
Rods
  pressure, applying, 124, 126
  rigged and ready, 32
  selecting, casting and, 93–94
Roll cast, 96–97
Rolling tarpon, 79–81, 130, 132

Screw-down tarpon, 81, 83
Sieglaff, Zeke, 57
Skiffs, building/selecting
  gear, 52–55
  overview of, 45
  practical advice, 46, 48–49, 51–52

Skiffs, running
  boat slap, 61
  emergency repair, 65
  etiquette, 58–59, 64
  fighting fish, boat position and, 126, 128
  overview of, 57
  practical advice, 61–64
  rules of the road, 58–59
  tips from Pallot, 64
  turning, 64
  wakes, 64
  when not to go out, 56
Spawning, migration and, 14–16
Stanford's, 45
Stump Pass, 4

Tiger Mouse fly pattern, 39
Tippet. *See* Class tippet
Tripp, Scott, 4, 6
Turning your skiff, 64

Underhand cast, 96
University of Miami Bonefish Research Project, 15

Wakes, 64
Water (for drinking), 54
Weeki Wachee Springs, 13
Weighing in, 140–141

Zarra Spook, 42, 93